PRAISE FOR

MAKING DISCIPLES

Ralph writes as a pastor who has a global vision. His church has planted 70 churches, and he is the catalyst for a movement of around 700 churches on every continent. For Ralph, making disciples is about who you are and what you do, and this book is filled with stories and cases studies from Ralph's own experience. The most important lesson I learned was that we can do this, and we can start right now.

Steve Addison
Author of *What Jesus Started: Joining the Movement, Changing the World*

The Western Church needs a radical intervention to reverse its current trend of decline. Ralph Moore is a modern-day prophet whose direct and, at times, abrasive style will work like sandpaper to peel back the layers that prevent the Church from fulfilling its mission. He calls us out in a righteous way, back to discipleship, and I applaud him for it.

Glenn Burris, Jr.
President of The Foursquare Church

The fruit of an emphasis on intentional disciplemaking—a movement of 700 congregations since 1971—speaks for itself and uniquely qualifies Ralph Moore to write on this topic. Designed for ordinary believers, this practical and inspiring book describes principles that, if implemented, will result in new followers of Jesus and healthy, multiplying churches. It is a challenging read that will help all understand that making converts isn't the same as making disciples.

Tony and Felicity Dale
Founders of *House2House* Magazine and Authors of
Small is Big! (with George Barna) and *An Army of Ordinary People*

Ralph knows that disciplemaking is core to church planting and God's mission, and he has the practical know-how to share this truth through compelling stories that illustrate how disciplemaking happens. His stories are filled with truth from the Bible, led by the Spirit, and focus on the essential ingredient of disciplemaking: building relationships. I urge you to read this book, drink deeply from Ralph's wisdom, and begin reproducing disciples to fulfill the Lord's vision for your life!

Joseph W. Handley, Jr.
President of Asian Access

Ralph Moore is a leader who doesn't set his smartphone navigator on the revivals of the past but looks at the decidedly non-sexy craft of discipleship. Doing the journeyman work of a gospel preacher, Ralph does the right thing in focusing on this most important insight: the individuals we are discipling are more than worth the trouble, regardless of the outcome or results. Do not miss this book. Keep the main thing the main thing!

David Housholder
Author of *The Blackberry Bush*
Pastor of Robinwood Church, Huntington Beach, California

Ralph's uncanny ability to see potential in an ordinary person like myself and others is a gift from the Lord, but it also comes from his intentional approach to look beyond what others see and to probe where others might not care to explore. *Making Disciples* takes the mystery and program out of the process and puts it back into the hands of us all. It's a simple title for a simple process. That's how you leave a legacy like Ralph Moore.

Mike Kai
Pastor of Hope Chapel West Oahu, Hawaii
Author of *The Pound for Pound Principle*

In *Making Disciples*, Ralph shares great stories and gives fresh inspiration and insight for building disciplemaking churches that reproduce and change people's lives. He believes every healthy church reproduces more churches, every passionate leader reproduces more leaders, and every fully devoted disciple of Jesus makes more disciples—and tells how we can all do that. Great job, Ralph!

Floyd McClung
Author and Founder of All Nations

Simple. Biblical. Practical. Ralph Moore's books are some of the finest discipleship, leadership and church-planting tools available today. Like all great writers, Ralph's life tells the same story as his books. If you want to be equipped and inspired to be a disciple and make disciples, *Making Disciples* is for you!

Steve Murrell
Founder of Victory-Manila
Co-founder of Every Nation Churches and Ministries
Author of *WikiChurch*

Making disciples is everybody's business. Ralph Moore's genius for realness and simplicity makes me want to go and make disciples right now—in fact, more than ever before. Everybody *should* do it. Everybody *can* do it. And, in this book, Ralph Moore strips away the fluff, drills down to stuff and teaches us *how* to do it. Read it, and you'll want to *get* to it! Buy a bunch and spread the word!

Norman Nakanishi
Senior Pastor of Grace Bible Church, Pearlside, Hawaii

I love making disciples in Japan, so I was so excited to read Ralph Moore's book on discipleship in the local church. Pastor Ralph is not only a great pastor but also a great developer of pastors and church planters. He is the real deal! This book will motivate you and give you practical how-to's in making disciples.

Rod Plummer
Pastor of Jesus Lifehouse International Churches in Japan

Based on the amazing work Ralph has done in seeing countless people begin to believe in Jesus, and then launching scads of new churches, he is on my short list of living heroes. Ralph just might be the most capable voice you'll connect with in this life regarding the development and care of disciples. As I read this book, only one regret occurred to me: *Making Disciples* should have been written a few decades ago when I first started to follow Jesus!

Steve Sjogren
Church Planter and Author of *Conspiracy of Kindness*

Ralph is the real deal. He walks the talk, lives the life and is a passionate discipler who believes that discipleship is the only way. It is Plan A, and there is no Plan B. This is the true and urgent need for the hour. We need an army of disciples and disciplers, and Ralph knows this business.

Yang Tuck Yoong
Senior Pastor of Cornerstone Community Church, Singapore

RALPH MOORE

Author of *Starting a New Church* and Founder of the Hope Chapel Movement

MAKING
DISCIPLES

DEVELOPING **LIFELONG** FOLLOWERS OF JESUS

Regal

For more information and
special offers from Regal Books, email us at
subscribe@regalbooks.com

Published by Regal
From Gospel Light
Ventura, California, U.S.A.
www.regalbooks.com
Printed in the U.S.A.

Library of Congress Cataloging-in-Publication Data
Moore, Ralph, 1945-
Making disciples : developing lifelong followers of Jesus / Ralph Moore.
p. cm.
ISBN 978-0-8307-6539-3 (trade paper)
1. Discipling (Christianity) I. Title.
BV4520.M59 2012
253—dc23
2012032160

Rights for publishing this book outside the U.S.A. or in non-English languages are
administered by Gospel Light Worldwide, an international not-for-profit ministry.
For additional information, please visit www.glww.org, email info@glww.org, or
write to Gospel Light Worldwide, 1957 Eastman Avenue, Ventura, CA 93003, U.S.A.

To order copies of this book and other Regal products in bulk quantities,
please contact us at 1-800-446-7735.

CONTENTS

FOREWORD

As pastors, when we preach Matthew 28:19-20, we often focus on the "go" part and forget the "make disciples" part. Both are vitally important. The loss of a discipleship-centered strategy of mission will render our "going" useless, unless we take care.

Maybe you're a pastor who senses your church needs a renewed perspective on discipleship. You realize discipleship is not a program and that a new DVD series is not going to affect change. The pain threshold has been reached, and you're ready to take Jesus' command to make disciples more seriously than ever before.

Or maybe you're a church member who is personally wrestling with God's call on your life to be a disciplemaker. Maybe you're the only one in your congregation feeling the urgency of the call, but you are at a loss for how to get started. The loneliness and burden of leading in the area of discipleship is overwhelming.

Or perhaps you're a church planter, and the urgency of multiplication keeps you awake at night. How can you quickly make disciples who then, in turn, make disciples themselves? The success of the new church depends on this concept.

I've been in more than a few meetings with Ralph. Sometimes they are discussions—and he loves to discuss—but his comments frequently come back to the same issue again and again. He wants to talk about making disciples who live boldly for Christ. Ralph's passion for discipleship is clearly evident in everything he does, and now it's spilled onto these pages.

Pastors, lay leaders and even church planters wrestle with the Great Commission in different contexts, but the content of their struggle is all the same. The Church needs transformed people in order to thrive. Without disciplemaking, it is impossible to obey the Great Commission. So, where do you start?

You're already halfway there.

Making Disciples: Developing Lifelong Followers of Jesus, the book you are now holding in your hands, is engineered to recalibrate your thinking about the Great Commission in whatever situation you find yourself. This book is for the pastor whose ministry is stalling, and for one who's ministry is thriving. It's for the church member who wants to be a disciplemaker but doesn't know how, for the church planter who is starting a new church, and for the pastor who is seeking God's call through church revitalization.

The Great Commission extends to each of us, both to "go" and "make disciples." I pray Ralph's book will help extend the mission a little further through your life and ministry.

Ed Stetzer

Author, Speaker, Researcher, Pastor, Church Planter and Christian Missiologist

PREFACE

This book is written for ordinary Christians, as *every* believer is called to follow Christ and become "fishers of men" (Matt. 4:19, *NIV*). We are each called to make disciples.

Having said that, I can't escape the skin I'm in. I'm a pastor, and I will ultimately write from a pastor's perspective. For that I apologize, as I know that some of my stories will come from that unique perspective. My confidence is that you will adapt and apply the illustrations in a way that fits into your life.

I just can't escape the consequence of intentional disciplemaking, from a pastor's perspective, one that necessarily includes churches multiplying new churches. If we do our job well it is natural that some disciples should quite naturally grow into pastors.

I've tried to keep the book practical for all followers of Christ, but at the same time there is a lot here that I hope will inspire pastors and other church leaders. The whole point of the book is to establish what I call a "disciplemaking continuum," where every element of a church is about turning Christ-followers into disciplemakers. At its heart, this book is a *church health* project.

You can read it as a stand-alone volume, yet it also completes a trilogy when read along with two other books I've written, *How to Multiply Your Church* and *Starting a New Church*.

If you do read the books as a threesome, begin with this one and then read the other two in the order I've listed them. A church first makes disciples and then it prepares itself to multiply. Then it can get to the nuts and bolts of launching something new. Ultimately, we should find ourselves reaching for the prize of making disciples of the nations, a task that involves every one of us and will alter the outcome of human history.

My goal is that your local church will gain a global outreach. I live in the most isolated group of islands in the world—we are farther from the mainland than any other island. Yet, we have managed to plant churches on every continent. It all started with a simple decision to get very serious about making disciples.

You might say we're trying to copy Jesus. If you did, your observation would be correct.

WHAT'S SO GOOD
ABOUT THIS BOOK?

This book is designed to change the way you live your everyday life—and to change it for the better.

I'm hoping to teach you how to change the world one person at a time. You will discover that the Great Commission, recorded in Matthew 28:19-20, is neither a lost cause nor a hopeless dream.

You'll gather tools for everyday effective disciplemaking. You'll also discover that disciplemaking is not reserved for church meetings or for "professional" Christians (clergy). It is the *call* of God on the life of every follower of Jesus Christ.

There are both purpose and mission in disciplemaking. We read in Ephesians that Church leaders are given the *purpose* of equipping God's people to do His work (see Eph. 4:11-13). If leaders exist to equip people for ministry, then the purpose of the Church and its disciplemaking efforts stretch beyond growing in Christ. Yes, the Church is meant to grow people in Christ—but not just as stronger believers.

The purpose of a church is to equip each person to strengthen and serve others. And there is an end-game *mission* involved here. That mission is to make disciples of all nations, teaching them to obey Jesus as Lord.

In any truly healthy church, most people will mature into strong local church leaders. A few will become church planters, and a select few will launch churches in other parts of the world. The Bible calls these people "apostles;" we mostly call them missionaries.

However, it is not only leaders who make disciples. Disciples make disciples—this is the most basic function of our faith. A man in Thailand recently pointed out that this is not about "apostolic succession," a term mostly used by our Catholic friends, which suggests that every priest can trace his spiritual lineage back to Peter. Nor is this task about apostles making disciples (though it includes that).

The man from Thailand coined an awkward but useful phrase when he said we are to involve ourselves in "discipolic succession." Of course, he is suggesting a long line of disciples making disciples—a disciplemaking continuum—in churches amid friendships. This disciplemaking continuum has proven effective down through the centuries. There is a direct relational connection that functions like a great chain that attaches Jesus and the apostles to you and me.

Incidentally, that man said the teaching, which you will read in this book, helped him to accept himself. You see, though he had planted nearly 50 churches, he has *no* formal education—and for that reason, he has always looked down on himself as inadequate. Once he understood that someone from America thought *he* was the real deal, in spite of a lack of education, he said he could "accept that God really is using me."

My hope is that, as a result of this book, you will begin living a more purposeful life and find that God can use you just as you are.

As I write, I am on a plane coming home from Istanbul, Turkey, where I met with missionaries from all over the Middle East. Most of them will never pastor a large church because they live in places where it would be dangerous for large gatherings of Christ-followers. Many of these people live in the very real and constant danger of losing their lives. Yet, all of them have this one thing in common: They are having *fun* making disciples. The consensus opinion among the group was that face-to-face disciplemaking is the most rewarding thing a Christ-follower can do.

I hope that your church, or other ministry situation, will shift into a mode of succession management where someone already helping do the ministry—someone trained by the person he or she is called to succeed—will meet every need for replacements in that ministry. In other words, I hope that your church will morph into a disciplemaking continuum. If managed properly, a continuum has the potential to launch ministries in the far-flung ends of the earth.

One of my friends says that "disciplemaking is the single greatest challenge we face in *filling* existing churches and *releasing* new leaders to plant new churches." You'll notice that he offers disciplemaking as a panacea for both the church that has lost momentum and as a key to fulfilling the Great Commission. My own denomination is pressing hard to regain momentum in planting churches. But I fear that in our enthusiasm we are overlooking the fact that only a strong wave of disciplemaking can provide the raw material for assembling new congregations. You can't buy spiritual momentum, and you can't obtain it through a programmatic approach to ministry. It must be relational in order to work.

If we don't grasp Jesus' simple plan of disciplemaking, we are and will remain dead in the water as a force capable of changing the culture around us. But we *can* be history benders if we choose to do it one person at a time.

In America, we're losing ground spiritually and numerically as we grasp for political power and devote huge resources toward building very large churches, all to the detriment of cultivating up-close relationships. The only answer to this loss is to return to Jesus' example and commission to go and *make* disciples.

Jesus said that you and I are the "salt of the earth" (Matt. 5:13). Then He warned against losing our saltiness . . .

You must wonder about saltiness when today's church is largely ignored in the West, while it is bursting with growth in the rest of the world. Why is that?

I believe the problem stems from a self-centered faith. Western Christians concern themselves with growing spiritually rather than equipping God's people for service. We engage in "in-reach" through what we've *called* discipleship while hoping that outreach will happen through our expensive, market-driven programs.

The result has been to change deck chairs on the Titanic. We are very busy attempting to serve the Lord, but we can find little net increase in church attendance, measured against population growth, over the past decades.[1] We're building bigger churches while closing smaller congregations, and the community around us couldn't care less. Could it be that we have too much money and too many great, new systems and programs? Our current efforts are failing to effectively raise salty disciples.

This isn't just a church program issue; it is actually a very personal process rooted in face-to-face relationships. Either you are discipling others or you are not—your life is poorer if you are not. And richer if you are!

What you will get from this book is some plainspoken Scripture and lots of stories about simple tricks designed to kick your personal disciplemaking machine into gear.

If I did my job well, you will come away with a new zest for life and you will enjoy some real spiritual victories along life's wonderful journey.

You will tread a path to personal fulfillment. You will make friendships that last a lifetime. And you will become a history maker, as will your church family. Your life will make an ultimate difference in the larger world.

If you buy into what you're about to read, you'll prioritize your life so that you find the time and find the relationships where it is appropriate for you to say, in so many words, "Follow me while I follow Christ" (see 1 Cor. 11:1).

Read on and learn just how easy it is to make disciples. There is no mystery involved in the process. You only need a love for people and a sense of responsibility toward the Lord and His command to "make disciples of all nations" (Matt. 28:19).

Note
1. Ralph Moore, *How to Multiply Your Church*, (Ventura, CA: Regal Books, 2009), pp. 27-28.

CHAPTER ONE

HOW A 16-YEAR-OLD

TAUGHT ME MOST OF WHAT I KNOW ABOUT DISCIPLEMAKING

The morning sun was already doing its thing as we sat on super-heated metal chairs in the church parking lot. I was a 19-year-old college freshman faced with the daunting task of keeping four junior high boys interested in a Bible story while sitting under the sizzling San Fernando Valley sun. My introduction to teaching Sunday School was no picnic.

Without the benefit of a roof over our heads or even the shade of a tree, about all we managed to do was make friends. Their names were Dan, Jeff, Dudley and Jimmy. More than 40 years later, I am still in relationship with three of the four.

Dan Boyd is the pastor of a large church. His brother, Dudley, is a successful businessman and Christ-follower. Jeff Miller is a church administrator. The only one I've lost track of is Jimmy.

CONFESSIONS OF A STRUGGLING YOUTH PASTOR

Fast-forward four years. I had spent the time in a Bible college where I carried a full load of classes, worked a full-time job and wedged in weekend time to goof off with those boys and others who joined our slowly growing youth group.

Upon graduation, I was a wet-behind-the-ears "theologian" with lots of fancy ideas about church growth and disciplemaking, while missing the very *obvious* dynamic of disciplemaking already at work in my life.

I read a lot for pleasure. One of my reading schemes included reading the entire book of Acts at least five times a week throughout my entire sophomore year of college. I studied church-growth books and bought curriculum for our church education programs. But I never really *understood* the power locked up in simple disciplemaking. I knew that it was something we were supposed to do, but it didn't seem all that important to me.

Strange as it seems now, once I began to understand the importance of disciplemaking, I still didn't recognize that I was *already doing* it. That's because I was doing it without any real intentionality.

My job description as a youth pastor required me to sit behind a desk all day in a church office (wearing a suit and tie). Obviously, not much was going to happen in that situation. But at night, and on Saturdays, I simply hung out with the kids in our youth group—and they were growing in the Lord. You might say I was getting paid to do not very much while actually fulfilling my job description during my free time.

I was a struggling misfit. I wanted desperately to change the world, but everything in my paradigm was upside down. Whenever I prayed about my job, my entire focus was on the programs we ran. The actual disciplemaking was just something that came kind of naturally and involved a lot of fun. There were serious moments and lots of opportunities to teach the deeper meaning of Scripture as it applied to individual lives.

But this was all informal. I would have never called those kids my disciples. I might even have thought you were a little crazy if you called them that; but in reality, they *were* my disciples. I may not have said it, but my life fairly screamed, "Follow me as I follow Christ" (see 1 Cor. 11:1). And the *time* I spent with them, away from church activities, was the most significant contribution I made to God's kingdom during those years.

LEARNING FROM A 16-YEAR-OLD

If my life was upside down job-wise, it was about to get more complicated in a way I could never have imagined.

My young brother-in-law, Tim, got into some trouble at school a couple of times. My mother-in-law was a widow, a deaf-mute, and was also going blind. The State of California, in all of its wisdom, decided that Tim would be better off living with my new wife and me rather than with his own mom. Worse, if we couldn't house him, the state would place him in the foster care system—not a pleasant option for any young person.

Ruby and I were just 20 and 21, and we had been married for only two years. We were still trying to figure out life, our marriage and my job. Life was no walk in the park, but suddenly everything got even tougher as we were forced to learn how to parent a 15-year-old kid struggling to make something of himself. We loved Tim, but we had little wisdom when it came to meeting his needs. We needed help, and we needed it in a hurry.

I remember forcing him to wear khakis to school instead of the low-hung Levi's with cut-off belt loops he was used to. We were hoping that a change of uniform would keep him from being accepted with the "lowrider" kids, like those he had spent time with in his recent past. We also helped him get a newspaper route so he could gain a sense of worth by earning his own spending money.

The paper route included a hidden motive on our part: If he earned money, we could then fine him whenever discipline became necessary. We figured that if he worked for the money, the fines would be more painful, hence more effective.

Both strategies worked. He caught on to the house rules so quickly that I doubt he lost even $5 to the fines. And the lowriders rejected him out of hand (it seems that clothes sometimes do make the man). This all came together in the form of pretty good behavior and few strong possibilities for friendship, except for hanging out with the kids at church.

Enter Dan Boyd. For some reason, Dan gravitated toward Tim. The class cutup in school, he was very outgoing and made friends easily. Dan simply focused friendship on a guy that was trying to figure out his world. (Dan was one of the original four boys that day in the Sunday School class under the broiling California sun.)

Tim and Dan's acquaintance burst into a tight friendship almost overnight, and it was only a month until Dan led Tim into a personal relationship with Jesus Christ. Today, Tim is a toy-design engineer at Mattel. He lives a solid Christian life, is an elder in his church and has raised his own children to serve the Lord.

I remember wondering why Dan was so successful with Tim. As I pondered the quick turnabout in Tim, I was faced with the sobering fact that the class clown had done something in a month that the budding theologian might have never pulled off.

The more I thought about it, the more I realized that Dan's secret was friendship. He spent time with Tim. Tim became his *disciple*, though none of us would have used that word at that time.

Being fairly bright, it didn't take long for me to put two and two together and reach four. Watching Dan with Tim, I realized that any real success I had seen in my own short years of ministry came more from hanging out with kids than it did from the programs we ran.

It was my own friendship with guys like Dan, Jeff and Dudley that God used as building blocks for ministry. Those boys and a couple of others (including Tim) had become my *disciples*. It was through them we enjoyed whatever growth we experienced. In other words, we were doing something right while looking for something splashier, because the real thing seemed too simple.

AN EMBARRASSING LESSON

While I was still processing the Dan/Tim axis, I met a guy who would drive the lesson home even further. He was a newly appointed youth pastor working in a gang-ridden neighborhood in East Los Angeles. His group of kids expanded from nothing to more than 200 in just a couple of months.

You need to understand that when we met, I was still pretty full of myself and my formal education. You also need to know that this young man had *no* formal theological training at all. That he wasn't properly trained only served to make things worse for me. I was offended—actually, you might better say jealous—by his success in spite of no seminary.

I remember pressing him for his program. I wanted to know the secret of the rapid growth he enjoyed while I was pastoring just 30 kids after a period of five years. This successful young man seemed kind of confused by my use of the word "program." It was foreign to his view of the ministry. Finally, he said something to the effect of, "Well, I guess my program is to get the kids praying, reading their Bibles and spending lots of time talking about what they've read."

His answer was a total put-off to me. I didn't want to accept that something so simple, run by an undereducated person, could vastly outstrip all the fancy tools I had at my disposal.

You guessed it. The Holy Spirit eventually got to me through that guy. I only met him on one occasion, and I don't even remember his name. But his example really stung. I just couldn't get him out of my mind. Spending lots of time being turned off by his story only made me think that much more about his words. Finally, I managed to link his success with those young gangsters to Dan's victory in Tim's life. After that, it didn't take long to discover that prayer, Bible reading and talking about Scripture were the keys to unlock some doors in my own life.

LESSONS LEARNED

The youth group in our church soon turned into a disciple-making machine. We were admittedly slow to jettison our fancy programs. But we added hanging out, centered on the Bible and prayer, to everything we were already doing.

A very dead 6:00 AM Tuesday prayer meeting for high-school students suddenly burst into life when we all started sharing "what I got from my Bible this week." That prayer-and-share meeting soon became the launch pad for an everyday invasion of our high school with humorous Christian literature and outreach in the form of intentional friendships. We grew numerically as the kids were growing into ministry. I was making disciples, and it became natural for them to make disciples of their own. Looking back, I guess that is what you could say of Dan and Tim—I had discipled Dan while hardly understanding it. It was only natural that he would disciple Tim after he brought him into a relationship with Jesus.

That prayer-and-share-the-Bible time was so effective that I recently got a Facebook message from a very godly woman who told me it is the reason she is solid with the Lord today. She is involved in ministry and says the reason for that is because I *made* her read the Bible every Monday night during high school. She went on to admit that during those days she only read her Bible on Monday nights so she would have something to say on Tuesday mornings. We brought her into the Scriptures, and the Holy Spirit caused life to grow in her heart.

Besides our larger group meetings, we organized several smaller Bible studies where fledgling leaders could learn to actually minister to their peers.

Not only did disciplemaking work with those kids, but it would come in handy a couple of years later when I became the pastor of just 12 people in a nearly empty church building.

LESSONS APPLIED

Not knowing what to do as a young pastor, I simply did what I had done with that youth group. I began making disciples of the natural leaders in the group.

I define *natural* leaders as people who have followers. If you have no followers, you are not a leader, no matter how much education you have. If you have followers, you are a leader. Some are reticent leaders, and some are even rebellious (they require a little more effort), but most natural leaders make great disciples and can multiply ministry very quickly. Our simple approach worked. A bunch of 18 to 23 year olds eventually turned into a very loose network of more than 700 churches worldwide.

Organically Speaking

While we were still a congregation of less than 100, we had 8 organic Bible studies that just sort of popped up into existence. I confess that I led three of them; and the fact I led three shows that I was slower than I might have hoped to be in to disciple leadership capable of replacing myself. (By the way, I am in the habit of turning a noun ["disciple"] into a verb, and I do it intentionally, since it communicates the process better than any "proper" term I can find.)

Virtually all of the early leaders of our church were trained through the disciplemaking efforts of everyday people.

Think of it: People became church planters who wouldn't be doing what they do without ordinary Christ-followers hanging out with them while the Holy Spirit did His stuff. Sadly, at this point, we still had no real cohesive vision for making disciples. This was purely the work of the Holy Spirit, and clearly *not* that of the inexperienced young pastor struggling to make disciples and lead a growing church.

Becoming Strategic

There is a Scripture that comes to mind here: "Know the state of your flocks, and put your heart into caring for your herds, for riches don't last forever, and the crown might not be passed to the next generation" (Prov. 27:23-24). Knowing the state of your flocks suggests an *overall* strategic vision. Without a strategy for moving people from followers to reproducing leaders, you will probably fail to win the next generation.

It is that next generation of leaders and believers that is so important to the work of God's kingdom. If you think about it, the rising generation is very important to you if you truly want your own friends and family to find their way into heaven. The next generation is important if you don't want to spend your latter days in a church confined to elderly people who are slowly shrinking as they pass away.

That 6:00 AM prayer meeting in the youth group and those eight Bible studies in the newly planted church eventually gave us insight into the state of our herds in a way that only personal disciplemaking can do.

We finally wised up and began organizing *intentional* disciplemaking circles in the church. We managed to back our way into thinking more strategically. But that is a fairly long story, and I'll tell it later in the book.

I may never have understood all of this if my wife and I hadn't faced the frustration of raising a young teenager while we were barely out of our own teen years. It was the wisdom of a very young man discipling another young man that led to whatever fruitfulness we've known in ministry. Dan Boyd, age 16, quite literally taught me most of what I know about ministry—and that is just how simple and effective a plan our Master had when He called us to make disciples. It works, and anybody can do it! Read on, and I'll show you how.

CHAPTER TWO

CRITICISM
I WELL DESERVE

Oops! I promised to teach you how to make disciples, but we won't get to the how-to part just yet.

Most months find me teaching leaders around the world about multiplying the church via disciplemaking. When teaching, I always struggle between discussing "how to" and "why to" during the limited hours we spend together.

Not long ago, I began asking event hosts to complete an evaluation of the time we had spent together. The results were surprising to me but predictable to my friends. The majority of the people complained that I spent too much time giving *reasons* for disciplemaking and not enough time telling them how to do it. They said that I always answered "how" questions with "why" answers.

While the comments at these seminars are generally pretty good, and we nearly always get several new churches born out of these times, this is a strain of common criticism. Partly, this aversion to teaching *how* comes from a sense that today's churches are simply too program-oriented and overlook disciplemaking because it lacks the appeal of technology and frills. In other words, there are so many how-to systems available that I don't want to add another.

In fact, I believe the *why* will help formulate the *how*. Architects often say that "form follows function." By that they mean that what you will do with the building should define the form, or the plan the architect will draw. The why is the function, the how-to, is the form that it takes. Why must precede how.

I also live with a strong assumption that if you decide to make disciples, then the Holy Spirit will show you what to do in your own unique situation. I am nervous about replacing the direction of the Spirit with the plans and schemes of a guy named Ralph. My fear is that if I spend lots of time teaching what to do, then disciplemaking will degenerate into just another gimmick. However, I will admit that it was reading the evaluations from those seminars that drove me to write this little book.

My problem with time spent discussing how-to is that making disciples seems so simple to me: spend time with people, include Jesus, and let things run their course. But I realize that some of my reticence comes from the fact that I am still an aging and unrepentant hippy, and that "just do what comes naturally" is not really enough instruction for most people. So, I promise you that we will get to the how-to part a few chapters from now.

READING THE CLUES

I can't escape my tendency to give "why" answers to "how" questions. For me the background information and the reasons for doing something reek of clues as to *how* to do it. The *why* usually deals with values and purpose, while *how* relegates itself to mechanics. The *why* will never wear out; whereas the *how* must change over time. Biblical values do not change, but appropriate style must constantly change in order to keep up with an ever-changing culture.

Innovation and Creativity

If you understand why you do something, you will probably never find yourself saying, "That is wonderful, but it won't work in my town." An understanding of basic values allows you the freedom to innovate. You can find a way to make something work in your town. Adapting basic values to new situations begets amazing creativity.

Toward the Ends of the Earth

The why of disciplemaking reaches back to Jesus and leads onward toward the end of the world. He put it this way: "Follow

Me, and I will make you fishers of men" (Matt. 4:19, *NKJV*). According to Jesus, the result of effectively fishing for people would be an effective witness extending from Jerusalem to Judea and Samaria and finally "to the ends of the earth" (Acts 1:8).

I live in Hawaii, which is just about as far as you could possibly get from Jerusalem, so we must qualify as the "ends of the earth." Churches in our state have multiplied new churches like crazy over the past three decades. We are the only state in the United States where church growth is keeping up with the population; so I guess we are living proof that Jesus' strategy really works.[1]

In addition, many of the churches in Hawaii have multiplied congregations in other nations. We usually challenge a new congregation to pray that God will give them an open door into another country. This door usually takes the shape of a relationship with someone from that country. Even some of our smallest churches have planted new churches by discipling someone who travels back and forth between here and another nation. One of the wonderful things about disciplemaking is that it doesn't cost much money. It does, however, cost time and love. There is an investment to be made.

I recently returned from Mongolia where I do quite a bit of work training pastors in disciplemaking. In preparation for the trip, I was plowing around the Internet looking for data about church growth in that country. I discovered that Christianity increased from just three people when the Soviets left in 1989 to around 3 percent of the population today.[2] When I traveled there, locals put the number closer to 6 percent. That monstrous growth took a mere 22 years.

The current annual growth rate of the church in Mongolia is more than 15 percent per year. That is good news. But what caught my attention was one blog that described Mongolia as "the end of the earth" due to its remote location between Siberia and Western China. It is not as far away from Jerusalem as Hawaii, but it is an isolated location and was cut off from the West for all the years of Soviet occupation. So maybe Mongolia is the end of the earth.

Ordinary People

I don't know if Mongolia or Hawaii really qualify as the ends of the earth, but I do know this: Much of the original ministry back in 1989 came via *ordinary* people (I dislike the term "Christian laymen," as we stand as equals before God) who arrived within weeks of the breakdown of the Soviet Union and served during the early days of freedom for Mongolia.

I am reminded that the disciples Peter and John were described as "ordinary men with no special training in the Scriptures" (Acts 4:13). The passage goes on to comment, "They [were] recognized . . . as men who had been with Jesus" (v. 13).

I know of a Baptist man who planted a church that grew to just six people by the time his money ran out and he had to return home to America. His departure left the tiny church vulnerable and open to failure. However, this self-appointed and self-funded missionary made one strong disciple during his time in Ulaanbaatar, the capital city of Mongolia.

One of that man's disciples felt called to pastor that fledgling congregation. In a giant leap of faith, he resigned his position as a medical doctor so that he could pastor those half-dozen people. Today those 6 have grown to more than 400 in one church, plus a cluster of other congregations planted by the mother church.

Another Mongolian pastor I know leads a congregation of fewer than 40 people. However, he travels much like Paul and Barnabas did. He's discipling young men across Mongolia,

Siberia, China and North Korea. To date, he has launched more than 30 churches. Think about it. This faithful disciple-maker can count nearly one congregation for every member of his own church.

I know of a man in South Africa who works with disciples in his own church and in adjoining nations. Because he is willing to father people in the faith, young men from other countries have moved to his city. He not only disciples these immediate followers but also travels up to 30 hours by car to spend time with his disciples in other nations. He is working hard at getting people to "imitate me, just as I imitate Christ" (1 Cor. 11:1). The fruit is a budding church multiplication movement. His work will change lives long past his lifetime and far beyond the borders of his own nation.

This is the "why" behind the call to be a disciple ("follow me") and the call to disciple others (becoming "fishers of men"). Disciplemaking gets the job done better than anything we've cooked up since Jesus called those men to Himself two millennia ago.

THE *THREE* GREAT COMMANDMENTS

When Jesus was asked to describe the most important commandment, He responded, "You must love the LORD your God with all your heart, all your soul, all your mind, and all your strength" (Mark 12:30). Then he added, "The second is equally important: 'Love your neighbor as yourself.' No other commandment is greater than these" (Mark 12:31).

We talk a lot about these two commands, but we seldom link them to the third important commandment—the one we call the Great Commission. It lines up alongside the other two commands in a sort of a trilogy. In fact, it removes the other two from the realm of theological speculation and grounds them in practical action. If we love God, we *will* want others to love Him. If we love our neighbors, we *will* want them to go to heaven. That brings us head-on into disciplemaking.

It is important to understand that Christianity is unique in this important threesome. Most of the world's religions are content to look *inward* toward whatever peace or righteousness a person can achieve. Most religions center on either karma, or self-improvement, or both. Only Christianity and Islam press their people *outward* to evangelize and make disciples. And Islam distinguishes itself from Christianity in that it recommends conquest, and even death, for people who refuse to cooperate with the evangelistic element.

ALL ABOUT LOVE

We are called to conquer the world. But that conquest is best defined in those first two commands—love God and love people. It is love that will win cultures to Christ. It is love for both God and man that motivates sincere disciplemaking.

We need to remember the rest of Jesus' answer to the lawyer who asked which commandment was the greatest. Jesus told a story about loving one's neighbor to illustrate this truth (see Luke 10:25-37).

The hero was a Samaritan, whose race the Jewish lawyer would have disdained. The hurting person was Jewish—a member of God's household in the eyes of that lawyer. While two Jewish religious leaders passed the wounded man without a second thought, the Samaritan businessman gave of his substance to bring healing to the man. He overcame the victimization of racial hatred, allowing love to prevail.

We are called to be like that Samaritan, not only materially but also spiritually. Materially, we share with those in need. Spiritually, we share what we have when we make disciples of them.

It is true that we are often surrounded with people who either ignore or perhaps actively oppose the gospel of Jesus. Yet, they are our neighbors. We are called to love them. We are called to lay down our lives in an attempt to disciple them into a living relationship with the God who is there.

We must remember that every church is supposed to be a missionary outpost. This is as true of you and your church as if you were to fly off to Tibet on a mission tomorrow. You are surrounded by a culture with values and traditions that are very foreign to the ones you hold dear. These values and traditions won't change nearly as much by preaching and programs as they will through simple time spent in close friendship. Your attempts at disciplemaking will be exactly the same as those of successful missionaries in other nations.

POWERFUL EXAMPLES VERSUS WEAKER ATTEMPTS

The stories I tell in this book are mostly about spectacular disciplemaking results. That is why I tell them—strong stories easily make a point. But truthfully, they mostly represent the exception rather than the rule. Day to day disciplemaking is not always exciting, nor is it always super-productive. The Bible speaks to this lack of excitement in a very practical way: "Steady plodding brings prosperity, hasty speculation brings poverty" (Prov. 21:5, *TLB*).

Unspectacular Results

Most people who invest their lives in disciplemaking will see solid but unspectacular results. Remember my brother-in-law, Tim? He meets regularly with nine young men, four decades after Dan first focused attention on him. If none of the nine young men do more than call a few others to follow them, you would have to call Tim's life a spiritual success. It might appear unspectacular, but it would be a success, nonetheless.

To see successful disciplemaking from a different perspective, think in terms of the entire population of the planet. Nearly one-third of earth's people *currently* follow Christ; if we would each make just two disciples, we could evangelize the world within our lifetime. If those disciples each discipled two, we could get the job done in a couple of decades. Think about this for a moment. The implications are real and worthy of your investment of time, energy and love in another person— even if the results of your efforts seem unspectacular.

From Unspectacular to Spectacular

Have you noticed that working with the Holy Spirit is kind of slippery? You never know exactly what He is planning to do with your efforts at anything, let alone disciplemaking.

I know one man, a machinist by trade, who discipled a friend into Christ, and then others discipled the second man into a deeper walk with the Lord and into ministry. The machinist has moved to another state and taken on life as a carpenter. He lives a quiet life as a loving husband and grandfather, while his disciple has gone on to plant 350-plus churches in Latin America. The first guy made one disciple; that disciple made hundreds of other disciples. Without the unspectacular faithfulness of the first man, thousands would be lost without Christ. The unspectacular produced spectacular results.

Some people are natural connectors, or networkers. They tend to make friends easily and usually know lots of people. They will produce a great harvest, like the guy who launched 350-plus churches. We need to activate people like that toward disciplemaking. But most of us are quite different from that. We are more like the machinist who discipled the connector.

Without the efforts, prayers and faithfulness of that one man, thousands of others would never have come to follow Christ.

We need both the spectacular results and the weaker efforts to achieve our goal. This is a game where *everyone* plays. Church should not look like a soccer game where thousands watch a few sweaty people having all the fun. We should all be all in, all of the time.

This thing called "church" is like a great, huge multilevel marketing organism. The difference is that we aren't offering material goods, but eternal life. And we're giving it away for free.

Notes
1. Ed Stetzer, *Planting Missional Churches* (Nashville, TN: Broadman and Holman, 2006), p. 9.
2. Caryn Pederson, "Running in the Spirit: Church Growth in Mongolia," Pioneers Media. http://www.pioneers.org/Connect/Media/MediaArchive/tabid/149/PostID/125/Running-in-the-Spirit-Church-Growth-in-Mongolia.aspx.

CHAPTER THREE

WHAT IS
DISCIPLEMAKING?

Well, what is disciplemaking, and how do you do it? I hate to disappoint you, but we'll still wait to get into the how-to part a few chapters from now. First, let's settle on *what* it is we are to do.

DISCIPLEMAKING DIFFERS FROM MENTORING

For starters, disciplemaking differs from mentoring. In fact, I think a misplaced desire to feel "relevant" has caused us to embrace the concept of mentoring in place of disciplemaking.

Mentoring just seems so twenty-first century, while disciplemaking feels old hat. Big mistake! We were called to "make disciples." Don't get me wrong: a mentoring relationship is valuable. We need mentors. But mentoring is a human shortcut when substituted for disciplemaking. It is not nearly as personal or as effective as disciplemaking.

I have had several valuable mentors in my life. We've talked or emailed on occasions when I've needed their input. But if we communicate five times in a year we've had a busy time of it. I see Moses' father-in-law, Jethro, as a mentor. The Bible doesn't in any way portray Moses as Jethro's disciple. Yet, Jethro included Moses in his family and gave him wise advice at a crucial time before moving off to live life apart from him. Jethro mentored Moses well.

It's a different scenario between Moses and Joshua. Most certainly, Moses *discipled* Joshua. The younger man accompanied Moses wherever he went and was schooled in both Moses' life with God and his leadership skills. Moses spent far more time training and equipping Joshua than Jethro did in mentoring Moses.

SPENDING TIME TOGETHER

Time invested delineates a crucial difference between mentoring and disciplemaking. Mentors are valuable, and there will always be a place for those great relationships; but disciplemaking is a different deal. Consider Elijah and Elisha . . . was their relationship one of mentoring or of disciplemaking? I think you catch my drift.

This shows up in 1 Kings 19 when Elijah was on a mountain alone with the Lord. He had run from Queen Jezebel in fear that she would kill him for executing the corrupt leaders of her personal cult. During their very private meeting the Lord called Elijah to anoint a personal successor and two men to become kings.

Elijah was a great prophet and leader. His prayers caused a drought for seven years. When he prophesied the return of the rain, the parched earth and financial hardship of the dry years nearly screamed "impossible." Before calling down the rain, Elijah overcame the prevailing cult of his day and saw to the destruction of its leaders.

Yet, at the moment of his greatest triumph, he fell into deep depression. God sent him into seclusion for rest and restoration. He then saw the power of God unleashed in a private showing at the mouth of a cave.

After God got Elijah's attention, He told him to anoint a successor, Elisha, and two men who would become kings over two different nations. Elijah personally called and anointed Elisha as his successor. But it was *through* Elisha that he accomplished the rest of the assignment. Elijah never got around to anointing those two kings. His disciple, Elisha, did the job. Elijah and Elisha functioned as a unit.

Elijah seems to have discipled Elisha quite successfully. The Bible records two miracles performed by Elisha for every one that occurred at the hand of his discipler. Their kind of relationship was much stronger than one of occasionally touching base with a mentor.

In fact, when Elisha asked for "a double portion" of the Spirit (see 2 Kings 2:9) that was upon Elijah, he was told, "If you see me when I am taken from you, then you will get your request. But if not, then you won't" (v. 10). We have no idea how much time passed between that day and the day when Elijah drove off to heaven in a chariot of fire (see v. 11). What we do know is that Elisha spent that time living close to Elijah. And we know that Elijah was willing to spend the time with his disciple.

Jesus, much like Moses or Elijah, lived with His disciples. It is both the time and the emotions invested that distinguish disciplemaking from all other training methods.

DEFINITION TIME

Here is my definition of disciplemaking: "Disciplemaking is an *intentional* friendship with another person, with Jesus at its core." This involves more than imparting intellectual knowledge of the Bible or even of God. For this reason disciplemaking takes a person to places he or she could never go in a classroom situation.

Disciplemaking invades personal space. You share your own failings, victories and insights with another person. A good disciplemaker invites his disciple to help with ministry, then do ministry on his own while the disciplemaker applauds the effort. Disciplemaking calls a person to do things he or she never thought possible. It aids in the fulfillment of God's vision and dreams in the one you disciple.

Maturity and Reproduction

Disciplemaking targets the goal of Christian maturity—*if* you define maturity as the ability to *reproduce* yourself. Again, this is not about gathering facts but about getting caught up in the net of fishing for men and women. If I make a disciple who does not disciple others, then I am a failure. This process is all about reproduction and multiplication.

The Heart of a Disciplemaker

Paul described the heart behind making disciples when he wrote to the leaders at Thessalonica, "And you know that we treated each of you as a father treats his own children . . . and urged you to live your lives in a way that God would consider worthy. For he called you to share in his Kingdom and glory" (1 Thess. 2:11-12).

We share in His kingdom and glory as we find a few people whom we can call our disciples. We do best when we treat our disciples as a loving father or mother treats his or her own children. Our goal is to personally introduce our disciples to our Father's kingdom and glory. It has to be personal or it won't work.

A MASSIVE GOAL

Jesus told us to press into the Holy Spirit for power to become witnesses to the ends of the earth. He also said we are to "go and make disciples of all the nations, baptizing them in the name of the Father and the Son and the Holy Spirit" (Matt. 28:19).

We must fully understand the "ends of the earth" deal— He surely wants every nation to hear the gospel. But I think He expects more of us than a simple *hearing* of the good news.

I believe that we severely misunderstand the part about making disciples of all the nations. It's not about making a few converts in a few nations, or a few converts in every nation. This is about *world dominion*. Not political domination, but the heart-level dominion of a God who defines Himself as love.

In other words, the mission is to fill the hearts of *all* people, *everywhere,* with the love of God who created them.

Baptism: A Relational Strategy

Baptism suggests relationship, and it is closely linked with discipleship. Baptism is a declaration of spiritual death followed by spiritual resurrection, or a transformed life. But what characterizes that life? What are we baptized into? Well, we get baptized into something called the Church—a relationship that people enjoy with others while they worship God. More than that, we are baptized into Christ. We become one with Him in His death and resurrection life. This implies a personal relationship in which we enjoy easy-speaking terms with the Son of the Creator.

More Than Church Attendance

While church attendance is acceptable in most cultures, baptism is the deal breaker. Even most anti-Christian cultures will tolerate a lukewarm conversion, but the persecution often begins when a person gets baptized. Whether it involves execution in a more fanatical situation in some countries, or something more benign like losing a job, baptism clearly marks a person as having allegiance to a Kingdom that differs from the accepted culture.

Anti-Christian cultures seem to understand innately that the Church is a people called out of a surrounding culture into a relationship called the "kingdom of God." Kings demand allegiance, loyalty and obedience. So a person's new allegiance separates a Christ-follower from those around him, creating a threat to earthly kingdoms and cultures.

Jesus defined this Kingdom when He defined love as obedience—"When you obey my commandments, you remain in my love, just as I obey my Father's commandments and remain in his love" (John 15:10). This membership in heaven's kingdom is not a touchy-feely thing. It calls for allegiance, loyalty and obedience. It is demanding. Christ's kingdom is set apart from all others, yet it remains an integral part of them as its members are called to become better citizens of their earthly kingdoms.

Baptism suggests a walk with God that is out in the open and on display within the surrounding culture. In our church, we often baptize at the beach, and there is no chance that people on the shore will mistake the act of baptism for some kind of water sport—baptism is so unique that it immediately marks a person, separating him or her from the surrounding community.

Did you notice that the Trinity is mentioned in the baptism experience (see Matt. 28:19)? This suggests that discipling includes a relational kind of faith—one involving the person of the Holy Spirit as well as the Father and Son. Pastor and author Francis Chan has written a wonderful book called *The Forgotten God*.[1] The title pretty well summarizes the last couple of decades in Western Church history. We've built big churches around exciting programs but somehow left out the relational/experiential part of our faith. One of my friends points out that the Holy Spirit is so neglected that He even gets left out of the cuss words.[2]

So head knowledge is never sufficient to describe disciplemaking, though head knowledge is certainly a part of it, because Jesus included teaching in His instructions, "Teach these new disciples to obey all the commands I have given you. And be sure of this: I am with you always, even to the end of the age" (Matt. 28:20). But even when He describes teaching and obedience, Jesus mentions His personal presence—He is with us till the end of the age.

Therefore, our disciplemaking attempts must include communication with God through prayer that both calls out and listens. This is all about Jesus, through His Holy Spirit, being present when two or more gather in His name. If it isn't relational, it probably isn't disciplemaking.

REINFORCING CONNECTIONS

If the mission or goal is world redemption, the strategy works itself out in the simple process of an intentional friendship with another person that includes the person of Christ in the midst.

This suggests that the best person to disciple a newly minted follower of Christ is usually the person who most influenced the new Christ follower in his or her decision to follow Christ. In reality, that person has already been discipled to the point of a life-transforming experience with Jesus Christ.

In our weekend church meetings, when we pray with people who choose to follow Christ, we immediately ask them to contact the person who has most influenced them toward their decision. We ask that they contact their friend or family member that very day by phone, email or by just elbowing them in the ribs if they are sitting together in church. We ask that they inform their friend of the decision they just made and then ask that person, "Where do I go from here?" That question, all by itself, cements a coaching/discipling relationship between the two. That slightly different relationship will lead to spiritual growth and maturity in both parties.

Remember, Jesus did more than preach and teach in a formal manner. He spent a lot of time eating with and answering the questions of His disciples. He hung out with 12 select individuals and spent even more time with a select number of three—Peter, James and John.

Several Bible translations suggest that even the Sermon on the Mount (see Matt. 5–7) was primarily addressed to Jesus' disciples: "One day as he saw the crowds gathering, Jesus went up on the mountainside and sat down. His *disciples* gathered around him, and he began to teach them" (Matt. 5:1-2, emphasis added). If you carefully examine the text, it seems that Jesus actually retreated from the crowds in order to deliver these wondrous instructions to the Twelve. It appears natural that the crowds followed, but the intent toward intimacy was with a select group.

REAL LOVE

The Bible tells us, "We know what real love is because Jesus gave up his life for us. So we also ought to give up our lives for our brothers and sisters" (1 John 3:16). When it says those words, it isn't asking you to die for someone else's sins. It is calling you to lay down your life while living much like Jesus did. The overriding discipline of His life was that of making disciples—He laid down His time, energy and emotions for them. He's asking the same of you and me.

Jesus taught His disciples to pray by praying with them. He taught them to heal by healing others in their presence. He taught values through His parables and in His ongoing conflicts with the religious elite. After demonstrating *what* to do, He sent His disciples on outreach missions of their own. He also showered them with approval when they returned. His strategy for winning the world was to spend time with a few chosen people, developing them into reproductions of Himself—hence the term "Christian," or "little Christ," later coined in Antioch (see Acts 11:26).

INTENTIONAL REVIVAL

It is whenever the Church has hurt badly enough to abandon its fanciful plans and programs and return to the simple strategy of personal disciplemaking that we begin using the term "revival." Oh, how I wish that we could use that term to describe the next two decades or so! And it would be so much better if we arrived at revival through intentionality rather than by the default of things getting so bad that we are driven back to the basics.

However, God is in control of the revival business. I lived through one and can tell you that life was a lot simpler if not easier. I can remember being seriously depressed as the simplicity of preaching and making disciples began giving way to the business of developing church programs in an attempt to keep people interested.

Since that time, we've chosen to intentionally focus on just four areas for organized, whole church activity: weekend services, midweek discipleship groups, equipping people for greater ministry and serving the world both locally and globally, largely through church multiplication. We still have lots of other activities going on. There is a softball league and a men's fishing group and so on. But those are the result of disciples initiating these activities—they are neither driven nor operated by our staff team.

TACTICS CAN (AND SHOULD) VARY

Jesus' tactics varied widely. He spoke to large crowds, spent much time with His disciples and confronted religious hypocrisy. He healed people and cast out demons. But His varied tactics all linked together in a continuum. Each part fit with all the other parts, pointing toward a common goal—the kingdom of God.

In order to reach nations at "the ends of the earth," Jesus first gathered a substantial crowd then culled out all but a few people. Settling on 12 men and a few women, he singled out just three—Peter, James and John—for His inner circle. From these few, He launched the *greatest* movement in human history.

Unfortunately, we see no evidence in the book of Acts that these three, who were closest to Jesus, engaged in disciplemaking the way He did. They must have made disciples, but if they did, their activity is not recorded in Acts. We do see a natural progression of growth in the deacons Stephen and Philip. However, there is nothing concrete to say that their growth was the result of one-on-one contact with any of the apostles. It looks as if the apostles were so busy running what had quickly become a mega-church that they had little time for disciplemaking.

It was left to a Christ-hater named Saul to imitate Jesus as a disciplemaker. He would first get knocked off his horse, see a vision and hear the voice of Jesus in a scary conversion experience while on his way to persecute Christians in Syria. During this frightening event, Saul was told that while in Damascus he would be shown what he *must* do. It follows that at least some of what he was shown was the strong validity of imitating Jesus by making disciples. Saul had plenty of knowledge of the early Christians and may have even seen Jesus before the crucifixion. He would easily have been aware of Jesus' strategy and methods.

Later nicknamed Paul, he figures so strongly in the book of Acts that it might well have been called "The Acts of *an* Apostle." He takes center stage in 21 chapters of the book. Contrast this to the fact that Peter appears in only 11 chapters, while James shows up in just 3, and John in only 4. It was Paul of whom Luke describes in Acts as always traveling with personal disciples. He emulated Jesus as the others didn't, and as we should. Through his efforts, Europe was eventually Christianized, leading toward ministry that would reach the ends of the earth.

Paul seemed to follow a formula. Wherever he went he did three things: He proclaimed the gospel (often accompanied with miracles); he made disciples; and he appointed some of those disciples as elders or pastors to care for the other disciples.

Even after having been stoned and left for dead in Lystra (see Acts 14:8-23), he snuck back into the city and appointed elders. This act would suggest that he planted a viable church. It may have been quite small, but size has little to do with viability. Pioneer movements usually start from a small place. The people he appointed would have been his disciples—though he apparently had little time to invest in them prior to the attempt to kill him. My point is that he preached, made disciples and appointed some of them to oversee new churches. This was highly productive, and the end result was huge. In making disciples, Saul/Paul imitated Jesus. His efforts give us a clue to our own potential success: copy Jesus, it works well!

You read nothing in the New Testament about large auditoriums, marketing campaigns or the media tools we regularly use, yet I believe Jesus would probably have used them if He were ministering in Jerusalem or any other city today. However, I am equally certain that He would spend most of His time hanging out with a few select people. Meeting places, marketing programs and great music are tactical tools. As tactics, they are always open to change while the goal and the strategies of Christ seem unchanging. Tactics are quite fluid; strategy is not.

To understand this better, think of a battlefield. The mission is always to break the enemy's will to fight. The strategies are set before the battle begins, as are most of the tactical arrangements. But when the fighting starts, innovation begins almost immediately. This is because soldiers on the ground face unexpected and often rapidly changing environments. *Strategies* remain constant while the battlefield dictates the adaptation of *tactics* to best suit the situation.

An example of this would be the use of tanks in World War II. In the European theater, American tanks were smaller, more lightly armored and outgunned by the German tanks. While battle planners had intended head-to-head slug-outs between tanks, our troops quickly learned they had to maneuver *behind* the Germans in order to shoot at the poorly armored rear of the enemy tanks. Tactics had to change to exploit the enemy's weak spot. Yet, even as tactics changed, the strategy was always to break the enemy's will to fight.

What am I trying to say here? You are not supposed to and you *cannot* improve on the mission (world dominion) or the strategies (disciplemaking, baptizing and teaching obedience) of the Great Commission. However, when it comes to tactics, do whatever works—even if it means spending more time on the golf course, more time surfing or more time hanging out at Starbucks. Think about whatever Jesus or Paul might do if they walked the streets of your town.

GATHER, EQUIP AND RELEASE

Much of what passes for Christian ministry today is all about gathering—*addition*, if you will, while Jesus' strategy presses us toward releasing people—*multiplication*. We break our necks to build big congregations, gathering members and filling their heads with scriptural knowledge without ever honestly equipping them to do the things Jesus modeled (especially the miraculous stuff).

But even if we do equip others, we can still forget the part about releasing them to do ministry in other places. We constantly call people to come, but this is only part of the strategy. Jesus did say, "Compel them to come in, that my house may be filled" (Luke 14:23, *NKJV*), but His statement went further. That passage in Luke, when read in its entirety says, "Go out into the highways and hedges, and compel them to come in, that my house may be filled." We often forget the "go" part of the charge.

Our mission is all about saturation evangelism, which only occurs when we gather, equip and release our disciples to go and make other fishers of men. This works on a macro-level when we release strong disciples to multiply our church in another neighborhood or another nation. It works at the micro-level when we feel empowered and released as disciples to reach outside our circle of friends in order to make other disciples in our immediate community.

Multiplication really gets going when we create new disciplemaking circles. I recently visited a church that implores its converts to begin making disciples of others while they are still new to the faith and are themselves still being taught the basics. You can imagine that this church is exploding with growth. They operate in a country where Christianity is tolerated at best. Yet their growth is modifying the culture. Disciplemaking is simple and very doable—anywhere.

I have a friend in Israel who is a self-supporting missionary. Everything he does happens in small circles of disciples. He would be thrown out of the country (though he is Jewish) if he were caught doing what he does. Yet, he touches hundreds of people while flying under the government radar. Disciplemaking really can happen anywhere!

In order to multiply disciplemaking groups quickly in our church, we often hive off part of a group to begin another. However, this can be painful, because people are usually deeply bonded in friendship in disciplemaking groups. But a little pain is necessary if we intend to multiply what we possess to the point of saturating our culture with the gospel.

Hailing back to Jesus' three great commands, we must "love God," "love your neighbor" (even if he isn't so lovely) and "go." I don't think disciplemaking is complete unless I tell my disciple, whom I once called to follow me, to go and further the process. To the degree that my disciples make disciples, I am a success. If they don't make disciples, I've failed at disciplemaking. It's pretty simple, and very scary.

MISSION, PURPOSE AND A PROMISE

In our church, we try to keep our mission in front of our people at all times. We state it like this: "Our mission is to give people the best life possible by connecting them to God and His family and equipping them to get involved with what He's doing in the world."

As I stated earlier, we focus on our weekend services where we emphasize loving a stranger. Our focus then shifts to equipping that person as much as he or she is willing to be equipped, which involves our mini-churches. These are small discipleship groups with an emphasis on what God is doing in a person's life and a goal to equip people to minister to each other. We then proceed to send our people as far into the world as is appropriate, whether it is across the street or to serve in another country.

We do lots of ministry in our local community. People are doing laundry for the homeless, rehabilitating homes for elderly people, tutoring children and so on. That is all local ministry. On a global scale, we are deeply involved with Samaritan's Purse and Compassion International. We also have a goal for every member to go on an overseas missions team at least once in his or her life. Of course our end goal is the rapid multiplication of churches.

These aren't just programs to us. We work hard to be a global local church. We want to disciple our community while sending our disciples around the world. Admittedly, not all of our members are doing all that we wish they would. However, it's the people who take these concepts seriously—as in working hard at disciplemaking—who are having the most fun.

Someone once said that if you want real joy, find out what Jesus is doing in your town and join Him in that. Hint: Jesus is really into disciplemaking!

Notes

1. Francis Chan, *The Forgotten God* (Colorado Springs, CO: David C. Cook, 2009).
2. David Householder, *How to Light Your Church on Fire Without Burning It Down* (Seattle, WA: Booksurge, 2009), p. 17.

CHAPTER FOUR

EVERY CHRISTIAN
IS CALLED INTO THE
GREAT COMMISSION

"E very Christian is called into the Great Commission." I was actually surprised to read those words in the last book I wrote.

As I read them, the words took on a new meaning to me. I had always believed those words without giving them much thought. This time, I took time to consider their real implication—if we are obedient we each *own* a small chunk of this huge task of world evangelism. By now, you are probably quite used to me saying those words in this book. But when I read them, my own vision expanded.

That may seem a little strange to you, but sometimes we say or write things that are inspired by the Spirit and carry more meaning than we first attached to them. That is the way it occurred in my life . . . as I tend to see disciplemaking as a group process and, being a pastor, I am perhaps a little too congregation-oriented in my thinking. To think of the Great Commission belonging to *every* individual Christ follower was actually something of a revelation to me.

This epiphany happened while we read *How to Multiply Your Church* in disciplemaking circles throughout our church. The book gained a warm acceptance among our leaders. But our leaders represent a dichotomy. They want to reach the world, but they love their friends so much that they don't want to break out of disciplemaking groups to start new ones.

As I read the words, "Every Christian is called into the Great Commission," it hit me that this isn't just a call for leaders or even for churches. Individuals are called to go . . . and often they go while remaining in the same church. People leave the comfort of a healthy disciplemaking group to break out and start another.

Sometimes going is painful, costly or fraught with fear. Now, if hiving off to reach more people is just a nice idea, then we can choose to do it or not. However, if it is part of the Great Commission and is personal to each of us, then each of us should be willing to bear a little pain for the grand task at hand.

I've helped start nearly 70 churches from our own congregation. Those churches have multiplied to well over 700 around the world. Each time we launch a new church, I am faced with the pain of change. My relationship with a close disciple gets interrupted, geographically, and I will inevitably see less of him or her. I also lose contact with the other people who move away from our church to aid the fledgling church planter. Many times I am losing contact with close disciples and excellent leaders. There is a price to pay!

This loss of close contact is just one of the costs of making disciples. There are massive amounts of time involved. There are tears of both joy and sorrow, and prayers of anguish along the way. I think some of this might have been in Jesus' mind when He said:

> Don't store up treasures here on earth, where moths eat them and rust destroys them, and where thieves break in and steal. Store your treasures in heaven, where moths and rust cannot destroy, and thieves do not break in and steal. Wherever your treasure is, there the desires of your heart will also be (Matt. 6:19-21).

You must ask yourself, *What are the treasures I am storing in heaven?* I know that most preachers, quite rightly, equate this passage to our tithes and offerings. I am not quarreling with them, since I teach that myself. But I think we store treasure in heaven by the deeds we do as well. And I can think of nothing more important than obeying the big three commands that

Jesus gave us; love God, love my neighbor and make disciples of all nations. I don't know about you, but I want to find lots of treasure when I get to heaven, including many disciples.

DISCIPLEMAKING CONTINUUM

Now, if disciplemaking were just a pastor's job, things would be quite simple. But if we leave disciplemaking up to pastors alone, we will never win the world.

We will never launch many churches unless entire congregations are organized as a disciplemaking continuum where people without Christ are discipled into the family, discipled further into leadership and some are called by God and discipled to a point that they head out for the ends of the earth.

In our church, that disciplemaking continuum involves every *seriously* involved member of our church family, and it operates at every level within our congregation. Admittedly, some people come to our church as spectators and will remain so until the Lord returns. But the ones gaining the most benefit have fitted themselves into our disciplemaking continuum. Doing so necessitates paying a price in terms of time, emotions and even separation (all the time), or we won't get the job done. Doing the Great Commission comes with a fairly high price tag.

We create new disciplemaking circles by releasing recently equipped members to launch new groups. Better yet, the *established* leader often leaves the group in the hands of his strongest disciple and goes fishing for new people. We do exactly the same thing, only on a larger scale, whenever planting a new church.

This always causes the pain of separation, and we often hear people complaining that they fear losing contact with close friends. So we are faced with two choices—quit hiving

EVERY CHRISTIAN IS CALLED INTO THE GREAT COMMISSION

off, or suck it up and go for the gusto. Sucking it up isn't fun, but if we understand it as a *calling*, it gets easier, and it becomes exciting. A really lively disciplemaking circle is always looking forward to forging new relationships. A healthy group is hungry to see one more life transformed and realizes that multiplication of new groups is simply part of the process.

WE ARE *ALL* CALLED

I can find nothing in the New Testament that suggests the Great Commission is reserved for a few clergymen. In fact the New Testament doesn't make any distinction between clergy and laity. Both words simply mean "people" in the original texts.

We are *all* called the Church, or "called-out ones." The gifts and callings of God apply to every member of the Body of Christ. The greatest mistake we can make is to leave most of the work to a few of "God's Generals" while the rest of us sit back and watch. Maybe an even worse mistake is to think that the church will make disciples through its many programs. Disciplemaking isn't about programs; it is always about personal relationships.

I have a story that will show just how silly this clergy/laity deal is from either the vantage point of those labeled clergy or those called the laity. A long time ago, in a far away place, I was young and just learning the ministry. Those were the days when women were still criticized if they wore pants to church. It was a time when every male showed up on Sunday in a necktie. Home Bible studies were somehow viewed as little circles of people in rebellion to their pastors. The goofy list goes on, but I won't bore you . . .

One of our students led a young Jewish girl to the Lord. She began her walk with Christ unusually gifted as an evangelist. This had to be a Holy Spirit thing because she was leading

RALPH MOORE   59

people to Christ in her first week as a Christ-follower. Several of her converts were Jewish, which is something of a miracle after all the hurt the Church has put on those people down through the centuries.

On one holiday, her family went to the desert for a long weekend. Her parents graciously allowed her to bring along several of her friends (read "converts"). This was heaven for her—new converts and a swimming pool. You guessed it: this 15-year-old evangelist baptized four of her friends in a hotel swimming pool, with her unconverted parents' approval.

Sounds good so far, doesn't it? Sadly, it takes a turn for the worse. Her pastor got wind of it and preached that Sunday morning against rebellious young people thinking they could do ministry that is reserved for pastors and other leaders. In his mind, she somehow sinned by taking on the authority to baptize her converts. He was probably preaching about her at the very moment that she was dunking her disciples.

I hope you are getting a little upset at this point. It upset me, because that church nearly lost that incredibly gifted young lady. The pastor was a kind and well-intentioned man, but he messed up big time that Sunday morning. If anyone was in rebellion against God, it was he. This girl was simply acting out the Great Commission (in great detail). If he had used the sense he was born with, he would have rejoiced that a member of his church was doing what Jesus said to do: "Go and make disciples . . . baptizing them in the name of the Father and the Son and the Holy Spirit" (Matt. 28:19).

The pastor should have celebrated that this young woman was touching lives he couldn't. He should have rejoiced that she was learning from *him*. After all, he was a good teacher and had already become an important role model for her. He should have jumped for joy that he didn't have to do *all* the work in that church. After all, Jesus baptized no one, and Paul bragged about how few people he had baptized (see 1 Cor. 1:13-16). They apparently reserved the act of baptizing as a task for their disciples.

From her standpoint, the young girl should have been (and was) crushed that her pastor would criticize her willingness to live out the command of our Lord. She was never the same after coming home glowing that she had baptized four friends only to discover that she had somehow made the pastor's hit list in a sermon preached while she was trying to live her faith to its natural end.

Do you understand what I am trying to say? The Great Commission belongs to *all* of us. Its joys and its sacrifices are *ours* to share with our Master. When we embrace them, we tend to win the spiritual battle. When we shrink back, we lose ground. The choice, my friend, is yours.

CHAPTER FIVE

DISCIPLEMAKING
AS PROCESS

Disciplemaking is a process that begins *before* a person becomes a Christian. I call it evangelistic disciplemaking. It often begins with prayer.

Do you think Jesus *randomly* chose a bunch of guys to follow Him? Remember how He saw Nathanael sitting under the fig tree before his brother Philip called him? (see John 1:48). Do you think that *seeing* him was something supernatural, or was that just a figure of speech?

Do you see His words as a metaphor, or did something supernatural happen? Did He choose Nathaniel with intent, or was it an accidental meeting? What do you say about His words, "I tell you the truth, the Son can do nothing by himself. He does only what he sees the Father doing" (John 5:19)? I believe that Jesus never called anyone to follow Him unless that calling was rooted in the heart of God the Father. Jesus did what He *saw* the Father doing, and you and I should be able to do the same if we remain sensitive to the Holy Spirit.

WHERE IT ALL STARTS

Disciplemaking begins when the Lord shows you who *belongs* in your life, Christian or non-Christian. It continues forward when you move into that person's life, heading toward an invitation to "imitate me, just as I imitate Christ" (1 Cor. 11:1).

By the way, that person may not be someone you would choose on your own—you may not even like him or her. This is where "love your neighbor as yourself" (Mark 12:31) comes into play. I don't know about you, but I've had some pretty stinky neighbors. When I get upset with them, the parable of the Good Samaritan readily comes to mind.

This kind of love and leading might cause the Church to be a little less politically oriented and far less judgmental of its neighbors' sinful lifestyles. Long ago, someone taught me that people live out of their nature. If their nature is sinful, they will live sinfully. If it's godly, their lives will reflect that. We might just want to stop criticizing sinners for sinning and start loving them into God's kingdom. This is evangelistic disciplemaking.

We should expect people outside of Christ to think differently than we do. We shouldn't be shocked by their vocabulary or their values. Remember, it is on you to build the relationship if it is a calling from God. Relationship building often requires swallowing hard while keeping your mouth shut. Arguments never bring people to Jesus. Love does!

THE PERSONAL CORE OF DISCIPLEMAKING

Once you are in a personal relationship, you can begin to share life and your knowledge of the things of the Lord. We'll talk more about the nitty-gritty of that in a later chapter. For now, think of hanging out with a purpose—that purpose being that a person gathers all that you know, both intellectually and experientially, of the Lord. Meanwhile, you should already be thinking about helping that person disciple others even before he or she decides to follow Christ.

At this point, you'll want to hang onto the scriptural admonition, "Set your mind now on sons—don't dote on father and grandfather. You'll set your sons up as princes all over the earth. I'll make you famous for generations; you'll be the talk of the town for a long, long time" (Ps. 45:16-17, *THE MESSAGE*). In other words, we should be more concerned with our spiritual sons and daughters, or disciples, who may become future heroes in the faith than we are with those who have gone before us. Naming buildings and schools after bygone heroes is nice, but those grand gestures often distract us from the immediate task of building lives.

A friend recently told me that an older man once told him he needed to get his eyes off of his disciples and begin thinking about his disciples' disciples. This means he should be equipping his own disciples so well that they are equipped to bring people they had yet to meet into full and fruitful relationship with Christ. This is like a parent trying to raise his or her own children well enough that their as yet unborn (or even thought of) grandchildren will turn out well.

This takes time. Think in terms of months and years. "Time" and "friendship" are the operative words at this stage of the game.

Even the secular world acknowledges this. In the book *The Rise of Christianity,* author Rodney Stark studied the growth of the Mormon Church and that of the Sun Myung Moon cult in the United States. He compares their successes with those of the first four centuries of Christian history. He found that "the basis for successful conversionist movements is growth through social networks, through a *structure of direct and intimate interpersonal attachments.*"[1] He further observes the dangers that can obstruct growth, "Most new religious movements fail because they quickly become closed . . . they fail to keep forming and sustaining attachments to outsiders."[2] By closed, he means that the people draw so close to each other that the group soon has no room for newcomers.

Stark does not present himself as a Christ-follower, yet he identifies the bedrock importance of disciplemaking among outsiders to the success of Christianity.

SHIFTING INTO SHEPHERDING

Start with one disciple. Do well and you will soon have more to look after. The person who is faithful with a little is given oversight of more—this is a basic spiritual principle.

Jesus once told a parable in which two men doubled the amount given them to invest by their master. Upon their success he said, "Well done, good and faithful servant; you have been faithful over a few things, I will make you ruler over *many* things. Enter into the joy of your lord" (Matt. 25:23, *NKJV*, emphasis added). There is a multiplication effect in place here.

It is also interesting to note that the master gave the initial investment entrusted to the one man who produced nothing to the one who had produced the most. In other words he *rewarded* him with even more responsibility. If you do well with one disciple, you will be rewarded with others to look after.

A further thought on this came from my friend Mike Kai. He suggests the parable of the investments could go on. The man originally entrusted with two talents, who doubled the investment, would be expected to double it again to make eight, and so forth. And he would be rewarded for doing so. Mike goes on to make the point that we should be "always content, but never complacent."[3] If God allows us to double or even quadruple our production, we should still look to multiply it again. Do that well and you might just develop a network that impacts your world.

I started pastoring as no more than a two-talent person. In fact, I may well have been a one-talent guy who was smart enough to invest my life instead of burying it in the ground. All that has ever come of my life has come through investing in others—making disciples at every opportunity.

MAKING DISCIPLES IN GROUPS

Time is precious, so you should try to build disciplemaking groups rather than working with people singly. There will be times when one-on-one is the only way to go. But it only makes sense to disciple in groups—it is a better use of time and it allows your disciples to participate in each other's growth.

Jesus discipled in groups. He had the 12, but there was also the inner circle of Peter, James and John. Barnabas brought Paul and John Mark on the first organized missionary venture. Paul took Timothy, Silas and Luke with him as he traveled at a later date. On his third missionary journey, we read of Paul traveling with "Sopater son of Pyrrhus from Berea; Aristarchus and Secundus from Thessalonica; Gaius from Derbe; Timothy; and Tychicus and Trophimus from the province of Asia" (Acts 20:4). That is a group of six men—seven if you count Luke who wrote about it.

Again, disciplemaking in groups is the example we've been given. This group thing is biblical, and it works. I hang out with a single friend every Saturday morning at Starbucks (Jesus is in our midst discipling two very good friends) before heading off to meet with a larger group of people that I disciple.

I've noticed that our local Starbucks now has five disciplemaking groups from two different churches meeting simultaneously. When I mentioned this in a sermon, one of our church members approached me to say he didn't know I went to *his* Starbucks—I don't. He thought that because there are five disciplemaking groups in the Starbucks where he spends his own Saturdays. By the way, he leads one of those groups. Stories like that turn me on!

SPONSORING INTO MINISTRY

If you are actually and aggressively making disciples, chances are you are involved in other ministries. And you may have already been surprised to find that your ministry compadres sometimes show a kind of over-spiritualized reaction if you suggest bringing newer disciples into your ministry team.

There is a problem of perception where people often falsely assume that another person is too spiritually immature to join the team. Our church highly prizes the disciplemaking process, yet I often hear a litany of reasons why someone isn't quite ready to put his hand to the plow. A painful example of this occurred when Barnabas parted from Paul over Paul's refusal to accept John Mark on their proposed second missionary trip.

When I hear this excuse, I try to remind myself of Jonathan advocating David before his father, King Saul (see 1 Samuel 19:4-6); or Barnabas vouching for Saul of Tarsus to the apostles in Jerusalem (see Acts 9:27); or Barnabas bringing Saul into the leadership team of the newly born congregation at Antioch (see Acts 11:25-26).

Your active sponsorship is part of the disciplemaking continuum. And it is probably more important than you realize. Sponsorship implies conferring a meaningful blessing upon the life of a faithful disciple.

MOVING INTO MULTIPLICATION

Multiplication of individuals, groups and even churches are all natural elements in the process of effective disciplemaking.

If you do your job well it becomes natural to part ways after a time. You do this for the sake of multiplying the fun by passing the process into the hand of your disciple(s). It allows you go off in search of others to start the process all over again. Multiplying disciples, disciplemaking groups and churches is necessary if we expect to fulfill the Great Commission.

Rod Plummer is a friend who pastors Jesus Life House, which may well be the largest church in Japan. The church is massive and the worship exciting. The place is filled with young Japanese adults at a time when other churches are wringing their hands about their inability to reach this generation. When you attend a service you feel like you've entered a nightclub that offers preaching—exciting preaching. This is a thrilling church!

But the pastor says all the excitement is for naught when compared to disciplemaking. He says that people who accept Christ in the large public meetings often last only a couple of months. On the other hand, those who come through disciplemaking groups stick.

This church is rooted in disciplemaking. They've produced a couple of simple study guides for people interested in following Christ. These are tools for both pre-Christians and people who have decided to walk with Jesus but are new at it. The books contain a cluster of one-hour studies that can be approached in whatever order fits the needs of the learners. Rod says that people who come to Christ through these study groups stand strong and will stand until eternity.

The extra power in their system is that everyone who completes the study with one group is immediately expected to recruit a few friends and start another group. The church is growing by rapid multiplication, not the addition that comes through smart marketing. Jesus Life House is one of the finest examples of a disciplemaking continuum that you will find on the planet.

When I think on these things, I am reminded of Abraham: "When he was but one I called him, then I blessed him and multiplied him" (Isa. 51:2, *NASB*). That blessing of multiplication necessitated that he and his nephew Lot separate their flocks and themselves from each other due to the sheer numbers of their herds and the great weight of God's blessing. In doing so they multiplied their family into two families.

Or consider the process of surrender when "Paul chose Silas, and as he left, the believers entrusted him to the Lord's gracious care" (Acts 15:40). Paul was leaving behind the security of the Antioch church. But perhaps more to the point, the Antioch church was entrusting one of their leaders to whatever the Lord had in store for him. Perhaps it was a risky and faith-demanding moment, but it produced highly productive results.

This takes me back to where I started this chapter: disciplemaking is simple, but its very fruit can be costly. It takes intentionality to resist remaining comfortable. Multiplication is painful. But it is necessary if we believe we are each called into the Great Commission. Think of it this way: "If anyone desires to come after Me, let him deny himself, and take up his cross, and follow Me. For whoever desires to save his life will lose it, but whoever loses his life for My sake will find it" (Matt. 16:24-25, *NKJV*).

Whether discipling people into Christ or helping further the experience of those who already know Him, there comes a time to intentionally multiply your efforts to include other people. This often requires separating with people you dearly love to free them up to make disciples of their own.

Notes
1. Rodney Stark, *The Rise of Christianity* (San Francisco: Harper San Francisco, 1997), p. 20.
2. Ibid.
3. Mike Kai, *The Pound for Pound Principle* (Kailua, HI: Equip and Inspire Resources, 2011), p. 63.

CHAPTER SIX

NOT
"JUST ANOTHER
PROGRAM"

Did you ever hear of a gospel blimp? If not, you should have. It is a classic story of humorous lunacy.

The Gospel Blimp is the title and subject of a delightful book about a bunch of Christian nutcases who purchase an old blimp in order to witness to the next-door neighbor of one of the blimp team. After many years, this marvelous little book is back in print in the form of an anthology titled *A Voice in the Wilderness.*[1]

As a parody on human alternatives to disciplemaking, the book is a riot of well-intentioned stupidity. These guys want to reach one man with the gospel. One of the gang hears about a deal on a used blimp, and they are off to the races. Their vision grows beyond witnessing to one man when these guys decide to reach their entire city, maybe even the whole world—not a bad goal, just a silly tactic.

They buy the blimp, spend hours wrapping gospel tracts in colorful plastic wrappers, don their uniforms (yes, they even bought uniforms) and go airborne. The neighbor gets the full treatment, but he astonishes them by displaying angry hand gestures toward their loving attempts to *bomb* his house with hundreds of tracts wrapped in beautiful colors.

The story is too long to tell here—buy the book, it's worth the money (and you'll get to read other short but colorful offerings by its author Joseph Bayly). While I don't want to give away the whole story, I can give you the upshot of what happens. The owner of the house where it all started gradually stops coming to blimp meetings. His commitment to the cause of world evangelism appears to weaken. Then, to the moral outrage of his former partners, he begins skipping church to hang out on weekends with his non-Christian neighbor. They are even seen with *beer* in the back of the pickup truck.

The blimp guys go bonkers over their now "backslidden" friend. They try to reach out to him with a somewhat reproachful kind of love. Then—you guessed it—at a backyard barbeque the blimp dropout introduces his former partners to his newly converted neighbor who recently accepted Christ on one of their fishing trips.

Of course, they try to enlist the new guy for the blimp crew . . . (You really do need to buy the book to catch the rest of the story.)

PROBLEMS WE FACE IN TODAY'S CHURCH

So far, I've presented some good ideas and a few solid truths. But you still may not be buying my message. You may think this book is a little idealistic and out of step with your church paradigm. If so, I'm glad, because my job is to try and break your paradigm. Let's take a look at some of the real-life obstacles we would face if we really tried to get back to simple multiplication through disciplemaking.

The Problem of Purpose

Everyone needs purpose. The problem is that we often search for it in the wrong places. We often find purpose for ourselves by building our churches into machines.

You may not be into something as silly as a gospel blimp, but chances are you've invested an inordinate amount of time into something that promised "great things for God," only to disappoint you with minimal results.

One of our church staff members constantly points out that while most Christians sincerely want to grow in the Lord, many never will because they don't get involved with a viable purpose. He goes on to describe many who do find purpose in a church ministry but never hold their own ministry to any reasonable standard of accountability. In other words, "Did we accomplish anything for all of our effort?" There are "God ideas," and there are "good ideas."[2]

Too often we opt for good ideas that produce very little fruit. A healthy church is constantly pruning the vineyard in order to bear more fruit. A church without purpose is dying. A church with mere human purpose may be growing but will contribute little to the kingdom of God. A life without purpose is boring. A life wrapped around a misspent purpose is a waste!

The Problem of Magnitude

One difficulty with one-on-one disciplemaking is that it starts out so darn small. Stacked up against high-tech hardware and really big, audacious goals, disciplemaking can seem downright insignificant. Perhaps that is why we see so little of disciplemaking in today's churches. It doesn't appear to be all that effective at the start.

But one author described the problem of magnitude in terms that not only are poetic but also bang-on correct. He wrote, "Do not despise these small beginnings, for the LORD rejoices to see the work begin" (Zech. 4:10). Old Zechariah actually wrote about a pitifully small attempt to rebuild the temple in Jerusalem. But the word God gave him seems to indicate that God generally gets pretty excited about big things that come from small beginnings.

Disciplemaking can seem terribly small when held up against the latest crowd-gathering trick to come down the spiritual highway. But I think what held true for the Temple that Zechariah described holds true for the temple that Peter said Jesus is building with people as building blocks: "You are living stones that God is building into his spiritual temple" (1 Pet. 2:5). It took a lot of individual stones to build an ancient temple. It also takes many living stones to build a church capable of changing his-

NOT "JUST ANOTHER PROGRAM"

tory. Some will look like big stones with lots of potential; others will seem small and perhaps inadequate. But there is a role for each in God's living temple, the Church.

I recently got to visit a wonderful example of the importance of small stones in a great wall. If you visit Masada, in Israel, you will see the fortress where 960 weary Jewish rebels committed suicide rather than face slavery by the Roman armies after the destruction of Jerusalem and its Temple in AD 70.

What you may not be aware of is that King Herod the Great built that fortress. It included a magnificent palace and was actually designed to protect *him* against insurrection among his own subjects. What are interesting to me are the outer walls of the fortress. Perched on the very edge of a steep cliff, you have to wonder how the workmen dangling over the precipice managed to position the stones on the outer face of the wall. There is no room for scaffolding, so the laborers must have hung in space while tethered to a first-century equivalent of a modern building crane. It would have been pretty scary work.

Even more interesting than the workers' methods is the fact that the massive protective stones wouldn't be there at all if it were not for rocks smaller than your fist. They had neither concrete nor mortar to hold the wall together. The small stones are firmly wedged between their larger cousins, which provide the actual fortification. It is the task of the small stones to lock the larger ones in place and help them balance on that precarious slope. Without the *small* stones, the entire fortress would collapse into a meaningless pile of rubble.

Because of these small stones, that fortress has successfully withstood the ravages of time and gravity. It also held off a Roman army when it came under attack in AD 70. It has withstood the ravages of time and weather for nearly 2,000 years and continues to do so. Today it is a tourist's dream; but I wonder just how many stop to contemplate the tiny stones that make the whole thing possible?

I think our disciplemaking efforts are well illustrated by those stones in Herod's wall. We are, as Peter wrote, "living stones." Some folks are large, powerful and very much in public view. But most are tiny and nearly invisible to those who don't look closely. Yet, we are all necessary to the living temple called the Church that God is building through His Holy Spirit. Every time you make a disciple you contribute to God's great construction project.

We are not to despise the small beginnings or small successes, especially while we do the very thing that Jesus commanded at the climax of His physical time on earth.

The Problem of Speed

The problem with multiplication has much to do with perception. We crave speedy solutions whether we are ordering in a restaurant, waiting to have our car washed or desiring that our church make a difference in the surrounding world. Unfortunately, multiplying numbers of meaningful relationships always feels terribly slow at first.

We love quick results and fail to see how "Steady plodding leads to prosperity," (Prov. 21:5, *TLB*). Hungry for numbers, we simply fail to understand the power in multiplying disciples two or three at a time. Disciplemaking is much like compounding interest in your bank account; over time the growth curve will grow nearly vertical.

If you do your homework, you will come to see that virtually every culture-bending spiritual breakthrough happened because someone took time to make a few disciples. This is true of the dark side as well as the good. Just think of Marxist Communism or even the Taliban. A few committed people, well grounded in their purpose, will usually change human history for good or for evil. It is virtually impossible to blockade the efforts of a few highly dedicated individuals.

Think of Christianity this way: One man with three close buddies and a few other friends kicked off a movement that currently involves more than 2 billion people, or close to 30 percent of the people on the planet.[3]

I was once asked an obtuse but life-changing question: "What is the true fruit of an apple tree?" The first answer that came to mind is, of course, an apple. Then I got real smart and thought of another tree. Finally, as the speaker kept shaking his head, I began to understand that he was asking for something much larger. The *true* fruit of an apple tree is actually an orchard.

It would follow, therefore, that the true fruit of a Christian life is a whole bunch of Christians—an orchard. It would also follow that the true fruit of the Church is a bunch of churches. A large cluster of orchards owned by a single King might even be labeled a kingdom. I trust you catch where I am going with this.

The Problem of Habit

One of the problems with this book may be that its author sounds like a one-trick pony. I admit that I simply can't get off the subject. It rules my life. But another problem may be *you*!

It is not unusual for a person to spend his or her life living in a rut just because he or she feels safe there. You may be struggling with the simplicity of my message. You may feel that it somehow threatens your current Christian experience or the way the pastor whom you respect views church. Habits are ingrained and can become a real problem. All I can say to that is disciple-making is something Christ commanded and is the major strategy offered in the New Testament.

Some things are not supposed to change; other things must change in order for us to remain relevant to the culture around us. However, we can get so caught up in culture and a quest for relevance that we form habits out of those things that are meant to be temporary. Worse yet, we often fall in love with the temporary to the extent that we forget those things that are meant to be permanent.

If you are to make disciples you will need to change your schedule and your priorities. In other words, you must change your habits. If your church wants to become a disciplemaking continuum, some things will necessarily change. But those ruts in the road, which we call "habits," too often hold us back.

I recently heard of a church in Australia where the pastor hangs on to 1970s paisley carpet because the people like it. I'd bet money that newcomers don't fall in love with that old-fashioned rug. Your habits surely don't involve carpeting, but they are subject to change if disciplemaking is to become a life priority.

REAL-LIFE STORIES

None of what I have written can be taken too seriously if it doesn't bear fruit. Fortunately, it does bear fruit. We've started a small movement by making disciples. And there are lots of flesh-and-blood stories that color my message.

A Professor Becomes a Pastor

I recently ran across a man whose life exemplifies the long-term value of simple disciplemaking. I first met him when he was a young professor at UCLA. At that time, he made an affable hobby of teasing one of the young women in our church about her Christian beliefs. When I heard about the friendly harassment, I asked her to challenge him to go to coffee with me. He quickly accepted the invitation, ready to debate the reasoning behind my faith.

We met several times and had interesting, if somewhat combative, discussions about trust in Jesus Christ. Our meetings then morphed into a healthy but short-lived friendship. Then I lost contact with him for three decades until I bumped into him at a pastor's conference about three years ago.

This man informed me that I had *discipled* him as a pre-Christian with the result that he had become a Christ-follower. Not only did he follow Christ, but he had also discipled many others into the Lord. In fact, he had eventually resigned his position at the university to become a church planter leading a sizable messianic Jewish congregation. By the way, his congregation has multiplied several others as well.

It all started with a cup of coffee and a willingness to spend time with a single individual . . .

Silliness Turns into Fruitfulness

I recall a time in my life when church programs that were not working had sickened me to the point of despair. I was still a youth pastor and also directed the Sunday School for that congregation. It fell on me to run a large contest with lots of prizes and fun events designed to bring people into church. From there we hoped they would come to know the Lord. This seemed like a good idea at the time. But it fell far short of the vision of the leadership team.

The contest was pretty straightforward. You qualified for prizes by bringing the most people to church. We gave away a TV set in junior high, a *very* used Volvo in high school and so on. The adults could even win seven minutes in a grocery store filling their cart with whatever would fit in.

Our church experienced rapid growth over those five weeks (attendance more than doubled) only to shrink back to its original size in the following two weeks. When the prizes went away, so did the people. I was discouraged and desperate to see some authentic spiritual success. It may have been a good idea, but it was definitely not a God idea.

I felt that I had to see something real take place in the lives of people in my circle. Without substantial church growth, I felt completely disqualified for ministry. In my misery, I latched on to the meager fruit of that silly contest. The entire positive result was one young girl who came to Christ. Did I mention that she considered herself a Communist both before and after her conversion?

Because of her political activities, we could never get her to church on Sunday. This happened in the very political late 1960s, and she was usually off on Sunday mornings trying to raise money to support Fidel Castro or some Left-leaning cause. She wanted to make the world a better place and thought she had found the avenue through communism. Her idea of salvation was that a relationship with Jesus would make her a more effective Communist.

Reaching out to her felt like grasping at the wind. Trying to hang on to the single convert produced by that silly contest was terribly frustrating. The problem was magnified since I was on the edge of leaving pastoral ministry due to a lack of any visible success. In my weakness I devised a somewhat convoluted plan to connect her to the church.

My idea was almost as bad as the contest it replaced, with one exception: it included the concept of disciplemaking. Please understand that my tactics were born out of pure frustration— my theology about disciplemaking was still pretty shallow at this point. The plan was simple. I began inviting her to the beach every Saturday morning along with three or four hot-looking young male surfers. As you may have surmised, she came to the beach and brought a girlfriend.

The parameters for those beach trips were simple: bring your swimsuit, a towel, surf equipment and a Bible. We'd spend the day hanging out, eating surfer-sandwiches (bologna slapped between layers of white bread) and talking about the Bible. The Bible study was simple. Each person was asked to share something they got out of the Scriptures during the week. In other words, "Read a little Bible and you get a free ride to the beach on Saturday."

It worked beyond imagination. The original girl grew strong in the Lord. She soon began attending church on the weekends and dived into the youth group. She even dragged along a few of her Lefty friends.

We soon had a Christian group meeting daily, at lunch-time, in the quad on their high school campus. They chose to sit right next to the Communists, in a circle, singing to a guitar and sharing the blessings of God. Confrontation became an everyday experience. But in the midst of those dialogues, some of the young Communists became followers of Jesus Christ. Talk about spiritual warfare! It was in full swing every day at lunchtime.

Of course, the church youth group grew. In fact, it grew so strongly and touched such rough kids that the church elders eventually reprimanded me for bringing "those kinds of people to our church." So much for a spiritual awakening! But this episode does show the power of disciplemaking.

The story gets even better when you look at the numbers. That one girl brought 12 others to Jesus in the space of a year. Those 12 brought another 27 people, including some of their parents. That's 40 individual conversions in a year. Our failed and somewhat idiotic Sunday School contest wasted a ton of money and effort. It (just barely) harvested a single convert. However, that one convert—through aggressive disciplemaking—caused 39 others to come to Christ inside of just one year.

This brings us to where you fit into the process of growing the family of God.

FAITHFULNESS TO GOD

Donald McGavran, a church historian, once wrote that "anyone who would comprehend the growth of Christian churches must see it primarily as *faithfulness to God*. God desires it. Rather then gaining something for oneself, finding the lost is to become 'our service for Christ's sake.' "[4] He went on to describe our attempts to grow the church as *faithfulness to Christ*. In his words:

> God's obedient servants seek church growth, not as an exercise in improving humanity, but because the extension of the church is pleasing to God. Church growth is faithfulness.[5]

You can live out that faithfulness in this regard through turning your friends into fellow disciples of Jesus Christ.

Of course, McGavran's logic would bring us to admit that failure to make disciples equates to disobedience or a lack of faithfulness to Christ on our part. His words are a strong indictment against our entire church culture. The church world, especially in America, is more concerned with drawing crowds than with heavily investing in individuals. We must remember that we are all called to make disciples!

Notes

1. Joseph Bayly, *A Voice in the Wilderness: The Best of Joseph Bayly* (Colorado Springs, CO: Victor Books, 2000), pp. 50-89.
2. Craig Groeschel, *It: How Church Leaders Can Get It and Keep It* (Grand Rapids, MI: Zondervan, 2011), p. 42.
3. Philip Jenkins, *The New Faces of Christianity: Believing the Bible in the Global South* (New York: Oxford University Press, 2006), p. 9.
4. Donald McGavran, *Understanding Church Growth* (Grand Rapids, MI: Eerdmans Publishing, 1970), p. 6.
5. Ibid.

CHAPTER SEVEN

WHO SHOULD
I DISCIPLE?

By now, you may be asking yourself, *Who should I disciple?* That is a very good question to ask. I think that every Christian has a series of discipling assignments. They mostly come through your friends and family. These people form what I call a circle of concern.

Disciplemaking is, and should be, a natural process. Force it and you drive off the very people you care most about. Hide from it and they are condemned to a life without Christ and the fulfillment born of their own potential ministry to others. And please remember, this a *personal* thing. If you leave it up to your church, you severely reduce the chance that it will ever happen.

PROCESS ORIENTATION

Consider the recent story a friend of mine. It illustrates the fact that disciplemaking is a process, not an event.

This man has formed an intentional friendship with his boss. They often play golf together. This man does not press his boss with his Christianity, but he makes no secret of it either. His secret hope is to bring his employer into a relationship with Jesus. The friendship has been healthy but hasn't shown much fruit in the disciplemaking department. At least it didn't show much until last week.

My friend forgot that he was talking with a pre-Christian while on the way to a tough sales call. Without thinking of the possible consequences, he asked his boss to pray for him as he walked out the door. Upon remembering that the boss isn't yet a follower of Christ, he almost asked forgiveness for the prayer request.

Imagine his surprise when the boss responded with a similar veneer of embarrassment, "I want you to know that I now pray every night before I go to sleep." The boss hesitantly, but on the spot, prayed for my friend's presentation. That simple prayer represented huge and wonderful progress. And it showed the power of a slow, intentional and deliberate process of informal disciplemaking.

Leaking Your Faith

A woman in one of my disciplemaking groups is in training to sell real estate. Her trainer turns out to be a member of our church, though they never met until she took the job. My friend was amazed at how adept the trainer was at "leaking" her faith to those she was training. She said that the trainer tossed out just enough bait, in the process, that a couple of the trainees asked her for follow-up conversations on what she had said. When the trainees begin asking questions about faith, the process begins.

This is the way disciplemaking is supposed to work. It is progressive, process-oriented and often requires patience. My first friend came to understand that he needn't lead his boss to Christ as an event (think of a five-minute presentation of the gospel). Rather, his task is to slowly and steadily disciple his boss into the same relationship with Christ that he enjoys. Understanding *process* over *event* evangelism takes the pressure off of you! Where my friend drastically fears the high-pressure presentation (don't you?), he can easily proceed with a long-term relational process of making a disciple.

Five Minutes Is Not Enough

Now, I know that you may be arguing with me at this point. You personally accepted Christ through a five-minute presentation of the gospel at a church meeting or through the efforts of a friend. But I would argue that you are either the exception or the five-minute deal was only possible because someone else had already been patiently discipling you toward Christ.

In fact, I defy you to find Jesus or any of His followers inviting people into a quickie relationship with God. The people John the Baptist challenged were religious Jews with much knowledge about God. The same goes for Jesus—remember, He came to the house of Israel. Think about Peter on the day of Pentecost. He was speaking to people who actually knew Jesus and yet had called for His crucifixion.

If there is a New Testament master of rapid-fire evangelism, it had to be Paul. Yet, he normally spent several days debating the veracity of the gospel with synagogue attenders before they showed any real progress toward belief. These people were already deeply educated in the Scripture and held a common belief in God. There are possible exceptions, like the guy Peter and John healed at the beautiful gate of the Temple; yet even that man was probably already quite well acquainted with Jesus and all He represented. A person's repentance and faith most often come as a result of a growing awareness of God and His claims on his or her life. Evangelism is a process, and it requires both time and relationship.

I believe that if we could move all Christ-followers toward process-oriented evangelism, we would see more people worshiping Jesus. Remember that Jesus called us salt and light—both are rather quiet and operate almost without notice. Evangelistic disciplemaking operates much the same way. It is kind of quiet, and a person may not fully notice that his or her life is changing until he or she actually meets the Master.

WHO OCCUPIES MY CIRCLES OF CONCERN?

If we plan on discipling people into a relationship with Christ, it is probably best that we look first at people nearby. I like to identify people in terms of circles of concern. These may be concentric circles in that you are closer to certain people than others. But they may be more sporadic than concentric in that you are probably quite close to a few people in widely varying areas of your life. These are multiple circles of concern.

Do you know how lifesaving stations worked prior to the development of lighthouses? It is an interesting history.

Certain treacherous stretches of coastline took many lives until someone came up with the concept of a lifesaving station. A lifesaving station consisted of a few volunteers and a boat. These volunteers made it their business to rescue sailors whenever a storm would drive a ship onto the rocks near their homes. They operated somewhat like a volunteer fire department. They didn't concern themselves with the whole ocean, only those struggling nearby. You might have called their territory a circle of concern.

Though fire towers and, eventually, lighthouses replaced life-saving stations, I believe the concept still retains merit for the Church.

It Really Is Personal

Your personal circle of concern does not include the entire world (though that task still belongs to your church as a unit, which means a small part of it belongs to you). Your circle includes those in your acquaintance that God shows you to be your personal responsibility.

This obviously includes friends and family. But it may also include the clerk at the grocery store who you hardly know, or the mechanic who repairs your car. Your contact may be often or quite irregular.

I had an interesting experience along those lines. The lady who cuts my hair is a recent immigrant from Vietnam. Shortly after I discovered her heritage, someone else gave me a copy of

Rick Warren's *Purpose-Driven Life* translated into Vietnamese. I had the joy of passing it along and the thrill of follow-up conversations. Your task is to inch another person toward Christ before and after they embrace a relationship with Him. This is disciplemaking pure and simple.

This also involves filtering out those who don't want to share what you have to offer. We can't build a fire with wet wood. This is why Jesus taught us to shake the dust off our feet when someone rejects our life message. However, even wet wood can change over time if it is exposed to a nearby fire. The issues here are prioritized relationships plus time. You focus more intently on those who seem the most ready to receive. But you also continue working with those who take awhile to respond.

Taste the Love

Disciplemaking is partly about producing information but more often about sharing life with its joys and sorrows. Just be sure that Jesus comes into the picture.

Most people are hurting at their core. The antidote to that hurt is God's love through another person. Let them taste the love and they will thirst for its source. Even the Beatles sang, "All you need is love." That's important, as the Bible says that love produces strong results: "Overwhelming victory is ours through Christ, who loved us" (Rom. 8:37).

We live in a world severely lacking in love. This gives us a distinct advantage when we set out to be fishers of men. People who would never respond to preaching from a pastor, or from you, open up to those that are truly interested in them and their problems.

For this reason, asking questions can be very useful, far more useful than making theological statements. Everyone loves to talk about their favorite subject—themselves. More often than not, they will spend time discussing their problems with whoever will listen. If you desire disciplemaking prowess, start by learning the skills of listening well.

Listen Well

Everyone wants to be heard—truly heard. We're each a bundle of ideas, opinions and feelings. We often feel that our thoughts and feelings are never heard, or worse, get heard by people who have no interest in them.

Try asking your friend what she thinks about any subject you choose and then listen, really listen, and you've helped open her soul to the light of day. Bring God, or some subject that touches on God into the conversation and hear him out (keeping your mouth shut) and you will find a window into his soul.

And it gets better. When a person feels listened to, he or she usually wants to hear what you have to say about what he or she just said. Here is your open door to talk about your own beliefs and feelings about God or some subject that touches on God.

Look Down the Road

In the Bible, the apostle Paul gave some good advice to his young disciple Timothy. He said, "You have heard me teach things that have been confirmed by many reliable witnesses. Now teach these truths to other trustworthy people who will be able to pass them on to others" (2 Tim. 2:2). Did you notice the words "preach" or "witness" in that passage? They don't appear, but the word "teach" does show up.

Real teaching is often quite informal. A wise teacher knows how to coach another person to discover truth for himself or herself. That coaching often works best when it involves asking questions and sincerely listening without judgment.

My wife watched another woman move very close to Jesus in a group she leads. It happened as a small cadre of women mostly listened to her vent. This woman joined the group along with a Christian friend. She came embittered toward another church. She declared that she wasn't sure she could believe in God if Christians were so mean. She refused to say what had happened at the other church, but it must have been pretty bad for her to react so strongly.

For several weeks she would pretty much repeat the same things about the other congregation, always stopping short of describing what had actually happened. Then one evening, another lady suggested she purchase a daily devotional in the form of an app for her smartphone. The next week this woman came to the group beaming about how close she felt to God and how He had spoken to her through the devotional.

The group earned her trust through patient listening. The woman who suggested the devotional had held her tongue for six or seven weeks before quietly offering the help she did. Listening can be hard work, but it does pay off.

DISCIPLING INSIDE OF GOD'S FAMILY

It is one thing to disciple people who are still undecided about whether to allow Jesus Christ into their lives, but what about those already in the family? Here again, circles of concern come to mind.

Who do you know that knows Jesus less than you do? Or who knows less about serving God than you do? Who possesses fewer ministry skills than you? And, most important, who has come to Christ because your disciplemaking efforts brought them to this very important decision? All of these are the people you should consider inviting to follow you as you follow Christ. They are your circle of concern.

A Hospital Church

I like to think of a healthy church much like an unusual hospital—one where the patients eventually find themselves on staff helping heal others.

In this paradigm, pre-evangelistic disciplemaking looks a lot like the work of ambulance drivers, the welcome team reminds me of the admitting desk, and so on. The cool thing about this comparison is that, in this hospital, every patient is invited to join the team of healers. In our congregation, we expect every member to make disciples—we routinely ask them to baptize their own converts.

An Ice Cream Cone

One of my friends describes circles of concern by likening each life to a large ice cream cone—the kind that is actually cone-shaped without a flat bottom. He says the ice cream represents all the people in your life. That part that you lick off the top represents those people you touch regularly and easily. These are and will be casual relationships. You relate to these people on an everyday basis but in a shallow manner.

As you go deeper into the cone you get to the more important relationships. It is here where you attempt to disciple those that are willing to learn from you. But that last bite deep in the bottom of the cone represents the people most serious about following Christ.

These are the people who also happen to be most important within your personal circle of concern.

Living Water

You could liken the life of a healthy Christ-follower to a stream in the desert. There may be water in a nearby pond, but animals will gravitate to water that flows from a spring to drink from the very fresh water there. Jesus once said, "He who believes in Me, as the Scripture has said, out of his heart will flow rivers of living water" (John 7:38, *NKJV*).

You are that stream of living water, and Jesus is the spring. Those people who are attracted to you are those whom you are called to disciple. They represent your most important circle of concern.

THAT MOST SPECIAL DISCIPLEMAKING SITUATION

If you are a parent or grandparent, these relationships are perhaps the most crucial discipling situations of all.

God promises to do His part in the matter: " 'This is my covenant with them,' says the LORD. 'My Spirit will not leave them, and neither will these words I have given you. They will be on your lips and on the lips of your children and your children's children forever' " (Isa. 59:21). That Scripture offers a wonderful promise, but it suggests that we must pass on what we know of God to our children and grandchildren.

We must play an active role in our family's spiritual inheritance. Another Scripture states, "A good man leaves an inheritance to his children's children," (Prov. 13:22, *NKJV*). Proverbs is speaking directly to financial issues, but who would argue against a good person leaving a spiritual inheritance in the lives of their children and grandchildren?

High-priority Evangelism

The best gifts God gave me, aside from my wife, are my children and grandchildren. Along with those gifts came responsibilities. I pity the families where the parents are so busy "serving God" that they are unwilling to move their own children to the top of their priority list.

RALPH MOORE

When my kids were small, I remember lurking about until each of them did something wrong enough that it brought them more than discipline—it actually made them feel guilty. I'm talking about true guilt, not some legalistic "rules guilt" put on them by us as parents, or by society.

My wife and I waited until they *experienced* morality and all of its weight and then we simply and fully explained the gospel. We then led them to ask God for forgiveness and invite Christ into their lives. This was no plaything. We were taking them beyond Sunday School stories into a *relationship* with Jesus. We introduced them to real forgiveness as soon as they were able to comprehend real guilt.

Of course, we did read Bible stories to them each night and taught them how to pray. And we were also careful to include them in the spiritual, or even financial, crises facing us as young church planters. We counted on bringing the "faith of a child" to bear on our toughest problems. This often meant giving them information usually reserved for adults. We always prayed together as a family when facing the more difficult situations in our lives. And we were aware that our children had more faith than we did. The faith of a child is pretty well untainted by unbelief. We believe that early engagement in family prayer contributed to the strong involvement in ministry both of our children enjoy today.

Keeping It Practical

We tried to teach our kids, and today, our grandchildren, the practical aspects of life through biblical eyes. Money management is sorely lacking in today's society, yet the Bible is full of good advice. We created work opportunities so they could learn to save, and we helped them budget weekly needs against longer-term spending goals (usually toys). We would plan an annual family calendar, and at the start of each school year, we updated our family rules (such as bedtimes appropriate to the ages of growing youngsters). That document was always rooted in the Book of Proverbs and always posted on the front of the refrigerator.

There are other things to teach as well. I was a petrol-head when my kids were growing up, so I taught both my son and my daughter to work on cars. Later, I taught them home-remodeling skills. This saved them money later in life but also helped establish their sense of self-worth and independence. I've had to teach some of those same skills to young men anxious for ministry or just a healthy life but unable to fend for themselves due to parents who never seemed to get the idea of discipling their kids.

Today, I try to bring as much input to my grandchildren as is appropriate. They have wonderful parents, but there is still a role for the old folks in their lives.

QUESTIONS TO ASK YOURSELF

Are you personally and intimately discipling anyone? That is the big question and the starting place for all the others.

We often like to quote from the book of Luke where it says to whom much is given, much will be required. When we quote it, we often think in terms of money—if you have a lot you should be generous. However, the passage actually speaks of obedience, not just money:

> That servant who knew his master's will, and did not prepare himself or do according to his will, shall be beaten with many stripes. But he who did not know, yet committed things deserving of stripes, shall be beaten with few. For everyone to whom much is given,

from him much will be required; and to whom much
has been committed, of him they will ask the more
(Luke 12:47-48, *NKJV*).

Indeed, to whom much is given, much will be required, including giving away your knowledge of God.

The Big Question

In pastor's conferences, I often ask participants to get pen and
paper in hand. Then I ask them to immediately write the
names of their three closest disciples, without thinking—just
write whatever comes into their heads. I'm always thrilled with
those who quickly start writing, but I am also usually saddened over a few who just sit there with nothing to write—by
their inaction they confess that they are discipling no one.

My question to you is short, but important to the kingdom of God: *Who are you currently discipling?*

Other Important Questions

Here are a couple of other important questions to ask yourself: *Is Jesus even mentioned in my conversations with close friends? Do
my casual acquaintances know that I follow Christ?* I like to bring
the Lord into conversations with pre-Christians just as I would
with believers. If I've experienced an unusual answer to prayer,
I speak of it as casually but enthusiastically as I would if my favorite team made it to the Super Bowl. I try to stay away from
religious debates and simply speak of my relationship with the
Lord and how it affects my life.

How about your family? Do you find opportunities to
share your spiritual insights with your parents, your girlfriend
or boyfriend or your spouse, if you are married? If you have
kids, is your relationship with your offspring spiritual as well
as parental?

DISCIPLING TOWARD OPPORTUNITY

Then there are church relationships. I'm always looking for young people with potential to serve the Lord in unusual ways. I intentionally become their friend. Then I attempt to teach them what I've been taught, to whatever degree our lifestyle and/or their choices allow.

This is where we get our staff members. We almost never hire from the outside, choosing instead to work with those we've discipled into effective ministry. And, since we see our staff as a training ground for pastors and missionaries, discipling our staff in our weekly meeting has allowed us to literally wrap our hands around the globe. We have discipleship-trained pastors (with or without the benefit of seminary) on every continent. We once even ran a small congregation at a scientific research station in Antarctica. By the way, we put serious time into discipling our staff. The discipleship meeting usually takes longer than our weekly business meeting.

I close this chapter by repeating the toughest question I ever ask people (including myself). It is the question I ask pastors in the seminars I teach: "Without giving it any thought at all, can you immediately name your three closest disciples—right now?"

CHAPTER EIGHT

PASSING ALONG
MY PERSONAL LEGACY

I have a friend who nearly ruined his life by concentrating too hard on leaving a legacy for the next generation. A legacy, I believe, is the result of a lifelong investment in others, not something you conjure up as you approach retirement.

This man was a highly successful pastor for most of his life. But toward the end of his working years he got caught up in building his legacy. He took his eyes off the reality of disciplemaking and became entangled with ministry "hardware." He launched several new ventures, but none succeeded as his ministry had in the past. The resultant failures hurt his reputation and hurt his feelings.

His later efforts took the form of creating massive programs, including a publishing house, a school and a cluster of other ventures that no one else seemed much concerned about. The tragedy is that in his earlier life this man focused on discipling his staff, and he did so quite effectively. There are literally thousands of people on every continent who are seriously following Jesus because of his efforts. Those people are his *true* legacy. I believe that he will someday hear the words, "Well done, good and faithful servant" (Matt. 25:21, *NKJV*) When he does, it won't be because of a legacy he tried to create in his sunset years. He will be rewarded for years of faithfully discipling young people into positive ministry.

YOUR PERSONAL LEGACY

What about you? What is your legacy? Will you be remembered for selling more life insurance than the next guy? Will they remember that you had a bigger house than the Jones family, or that you waxed your BMW every Saturday morning? What will be your legacy?

You may be thinking, *I am just an ordinary Christian and really haven't got that much to offer. I have no legacy and am uncon-*

cerned about it. That is a lie from the devil. You have a great legacy to hand off to others. Your calling is as important and as valid as that of the most famous Christian on your radar screen. We are in this together, and we need you—desperately.

What Is a Legacy?

According to dictionary.com, a legacy is, "A gift of property, especially personal property, as money, by will, a bequest. Anything handed down from the past, as from an ancestor or predecessor."[1] I would like to state once again that we are not focusing on money in this discussion. However, in a way, money does come into the picture, and we should discuss it before getting on to the weightier stuff.

I recently picked up a slogan that is worth remembering. It speaks to the process of foreign missions (disciplemaking overseas). It goes like this: "Some are called to go, while others are called to give." So, giving money to missions, or even tithing to your church and its ministry becomes a method for passing along a personal legacy. Your money can go where you cannot. Just be sure you are investing it in a way that produces disciples who make more disciples, if you really want to leave a lasting legacy.

The second part of that dictionary.com definition reads, "Anything handed down from the past, as from an ancestor or predecessor."[2] You may not be the ancestor here. At least not yet! But you are the predecessor, meaning you have gone somewhere that another person has not. Your legacy is the sum of your experience with God as you hand it off to another person.

Try to give away as much experiential and intellectual knowledge as you possibly can. Teach others to pray for one another. Help them understand how to hear the voice of God through the Scriptures and through their prayer life. If you have a gift of giving, show others how it works and the blessings it brings. If your gift is administration, help others who don't possess the gift to better utilize whatever resources God gives them. If you are a leader, help others learn to lead. If you are a pastor, teach others the ins and outs of shepherding God's flock. If you are a pastor helping someone launch a church, be sure you coach him or her before *and* after the start date.

Reaching Back to Abraham

Each of us has a legacy. It starts with a personal covenant between you and God. Our walk with God reaches back to God's covenant with Abraham in the Old Testament. This is so important that the Bible calls Abraham the "father of all who believe" (Rom. 4:16).

God was very generous with Abraham and promised that generosity to his heirs: "And I will establish My covenant between Me and you and your descendants after you in their generations, for an everlasting covenant, to be God to you and your descendants after you" (Gen. 17:7, *NKJV*). This promise applies to you. As a believer, you are a spiritual descendant of Abraham. God will always be your God—that is His covenant with you. He will also become God to those whom you bring along with you—your disciples. Your covenant, your story about God in your life, is your legacy.

Your knowledge of God's secrets is part of your legacy. There are Scriptures that you cling to, and there are specific ways these Scripture promises have worked out in your own life. You become like that person whom Jesus described as a "homeowner who brings from his storeroom new gems of truth as well as old" (Matt. 13:52). As you unload gems of biblical truth from your personal storeroom, you deposit a legacy of spiritual life and blessing in others.

The psalmist describes these secret gems of truth in this way: "Who is the man that fears the LORD? Him shall He teach in the way He chooses. He himself shall dwell in prosperity, and his descendants shall inherit the earth. The secret of the LORD is with those who fear Him, and He will show them His covenant" (Ps. 25:12-14, *NKJV*).

God has promised to teach you. He's promised to prosper you and He's promised that your descendants will have an inheritance. He says His secret(s) belong to people like you who reverence Him, and that He will show you His covenant. I think this means that His covenant with you will show itself in all of the other promises made in that passage. Your secrets with God are part of the legacy God intends for you to share with your disciples.

IT'S NOT DIFFICULT

There is one huge problem with disciplemaking. I don't mean that it is difficult, because it isn't. The problem is that we often make it more mystical or complicated than it really is. The result of this problem is that people (like you and me) often don't pass the baton to the next person, because we feel that we haven't much to offer him or her or that our efforts are somehow insignificant.

A friend recently commented about our church and its outreach around the world. He said we were a one-church mission agency. I corrected him that we are simply a people who have actually *attempted* the process of disciplemaking in a wholesale manner. And we discovered that it works. Though we are a congregation of a couple of thousand people each weekend, we believe more in face-to-face relationships than we do in gathering large crowds. The result is that we've been able to tap into the awesome power of multiplication in all that we do.

As each person discipled two or three others, the disciple-making pyramid grew until we found that we were doing ministry in every continent. And we still manage to attract fairly large crowds. We haven't had to sacrifice at home in order to affect ministry throughout the planet. In fact, our weekend services have grown as a result of disciplemaking relationships more than they have because of our ancillary marketing efforts.

RELIGIOUS DUALISM

Overall church attendance in the United States was nearly stagnant in the last decade of the twentieth century and the first decade of the twenty-first. I believe that the problem of stagnant church growth in America stems from the way we do church. We practice a form of religious dualism where one group of people stands head and shoulders above the rest. We call them pastors, bishops or simply leaders. These are valid titles, and it is certainly necessary to delineate various roles. But we often label people in a way that suggests that the rest of the church is somehow inferior to them. This gets us into trouble.

Shiny Programs Can Get in the Way . . .

Our churches can overwhelm our members with great music, super graphics and high technology. This often happens while relegating disciplemaking to a very minor role, if any at all. Our shiny programs can leave our people unaware that they are even called to make disciples. Great music and attractive presentations of truth are wonderful, and we should surely put them to use. However, we must ensure that talent and skill do not crowd out that important command to go and make disciples (see Matt: 28:19).

A year ago, I asked a group of pastors of very large churches in one African nation if there is any part of Jesus' example lacking in their churches. They *all* answered, "Yes, it is disciple-making." One man even pulled me aside to ask if I could teach him how to disciple his youngest son who was still in his teens. He said that he's lost his two grown sons to alcohol and loose women.

This man pastors more than 10,000 people, yet he confesses that he does not know how to make disciples. The missionaries taught him how to hold large crusades, and he built a church around that model. He shed many tears as he unfolded the story of his life, church and family. I wept with him. Disciplemaking is so simple, but the missionaries never taught him its importance or effectiveness.

It is interesting to me that one year later I visited a much poorer African country. Every pastor who attended the conference is making disciples back home. Remember the question that I like to ask in seminars? When I asked these pastors to write the names of three people they were currently discipling, they *all* began writing immediately. They are disciplemakers.

I'm an outsider, and my observation may not be accurate, but it seemed to me that their very poverty drove them to do the thing that Jesus linked to church growth. They lack the resources to pull off huge events and are better off for it. I also noticed that the pastors in the poorer nation are heavily involved in multiplying churches—a natural outgrowth of disciplemaking.

An exciting side note is something else that happened during the seminar I taught in this poor African nation. I rather offhandedly mentioned the idea of house-churches as a tool for planting new congregations. We had already discussed the concept of a local pastor training church planters through disciplemaking without the benefit of seminary. It was apparent that they had already bought into that idea long before I came to town. But when I described house-churches, everyone began writing feverishly.

I asked the translator why they were suddenly so interested in what I had said. When he asked them, they replied, "We've just been taught how to plant churches without needing money from America." Somehow, they had previously "learned" that they needed a building and land to start a church. Buildings and land cost money that they do not have. Church multiplication was awaiting American dollars to overcome artificial financial obstacles.

When I say that buildings and land represent artificial financial obstacles, I am thinking of Paul and his compadres who, "On the Sabbath . . . went a little way outside the city to a riverbank, where we thought people would be meeting for prayer" (Acts 16:13). Later, the group would gather in the home of a merchant named Lydia that they had baptized in that meeting by the river. What worked 2,000 years ago, works today. In fact, we planted our congregation under a tree at a beach park because no one would rent space for a church.

The idea of a house or an outdoors location as a meeting place coupled with pastors training pastors was liberating for these African pastors. I expect the birth of a great many more churches because of our time together during that hot and humid day.

Godlike Status

The sad thing is that making disciples is the one part of Jesus' ministry that doesn't require spiritual gifts such as prophecy, healing, faith, teaching and so on. And, as we've discussed, it doesn't demand the expense of land and buildings. To effectively make disciples, you'll spend little more than the cost of an occasional cup of coffee. Disciplemaking is something every

Christ-follower can and should be doing. It is the very building material of the Church. Yet, we continue to ignore it.

One result is that we struggle with a situation that has plagued the Church from its earliest days. The Corinthians had this problem when they argued over which leader to follow—Paul, Apollos, Peter or Jesus (see 1 Cor. 1:12). They had elevated three humans to the same status as the Son of God. In correcting the Corinthian church, Paul questioned such behavior, saying, isn't this "acting just like people of the world?" (1 Cor. 3:4). In elevating the few, the members of that congregation depreciated their own role in God's family.

We do the same thing whenever we elevate our leaders to super-human or super-spiritual status. We depreciate ourselves when we relegate ourselves to sitting along the sidelines as spectators, or worse yet, mere consumers of a religious product. The result is that we fail to see the value we each possess to the kingdom of God. The Kingdom is smaller for our lack of understanding.

Connectors

Each of us is called to be a connector. First, we connect with people who need us in their lives. Then we connect them to God by sharing our spiritual secrets along with the tools necessary for a full life. We also connect them to other Christ-followers through church and fellowship groups. Finally, we will connect most, if not all, to a disciplemaking ministry of their own. And don't forget that we also must connect one generation to another. If we fail at this stage of the game, the Church won't even be around 40 years from now.

All of this is our personal legacy. I believe that disciplemaking should be the most important focus for any church. Everybody plays or we all lose!

Notes
1. "Legacy," Dictionary.com. http://dictionary.reference.com/browse/legacy.
2. Ibid.

CHAPTER NINE

THE "HOW-TO" PART

A bout a year ago, I found myself in a planning meeting with some pretty high-powered people. As we talked, I mentioned the words "disciplemaking continuum." One man instantly jumped on the term. He wanted to know what I meant.

Now, this guy is a famous Christian author and a powerful leader, so I felt a little intimidated answering him. I'm not given to inventing terminology, but these words are important to me and they form the core of our church's DNA. We feel that it is the reason we've been able to turn a congregation of 12 young people into hundreds of congregations (and still counting) around the world. When I explained myself, he nodded his head and grunted—positively, I think. But I am still not sure if I really communicated to him what is in my heart when I use that term. I'll try with you.

WHAT IS A DISCIPLEMAKING CONTINUUM?

The answer to the question, "What is a disciplemaking continuum?" is simple: It is a church that intentionally disciples people at *every* level and with *every* ministry in concert with all the others. This disciplemaking continuum spreads beyond our city boundaries. It grew into a strong missional force as we launched our disciples as church planters around the planet.

The ideal result is that each person in our ministry sees himself or herself as a link in the great chain of Christian history. The disciplemaking continuum views its most basic strategy as that of taking *every* individual as far as he or she can possibly go into meaningful ministry. After all, Jesus did not call a bunch of fishermen by saying, "Follow me and I'll help you grow spiritually." He called them to something greater than personal growth. His bid was for them to grow spiritually *to the extent* that they became fishers of men. They were called into disciplemaking in order that they might do the works of God—that they would be strong enough to make disciples of their own, who would in turn make disciples of others.

As Far As They Can Go

I believe that *every church* should integrate and focus all its efforts toward discipling every not-yet Christ-follower into a fired-up, slightly fanatical missionary. You read that right; I'm looking at every new convert I meet as a *potential* missionary to another country. To me this makes total sense if I truly believe in disciplemaking. Making disciples is often relegated to introducing new believers to basic biblical truth. But that concept falls miles short of discipling nations. We should be looking toward ultimate victory, a victory that is worldwide in scope.

I'm no fool. I fully understand that most people will never become missionaries or pastors. But my point is that we can and should organize our churches so that they represent a continuum or movement along a straight line rather than as a bunch of disconnected programs. Everything should point toward and support disciplemaking that reaches out to entire nations—after all, it is the third great commandment after loving God and loving one another.

The goal of every church and of every believer should be that of *inching* everyone we know more deeply into a relationship with God that ultimately brings other people along with it. We should take every person as far as he or she can go, as far as their spiritual gifts will take them.

Throw Yourself into This

We've already looked at this Scripture, but I think it is worth a second look. Have you noticed the *movement* in Paul's words to his disciple Timothy? "So, my son, throw yourself into this work for Christ. Pass on what you heard from me . . . to reliable leaders who are competent to teach others" (2 Tim. 2:1-2, *THE MESSAGE*).

First, Paul tells Timothy to "throw" himself into "this work for Christ." What work? Disciplemaking—Paul instructs Timothy to take what he has heard from Paul and pass it along to reliable people who are capable of teaching others. I don't know about you, but I count five levels of disciples in that passage: (1) Paul (a protégé of Barnabas), (2) Timothy, (3) reliable leaders, (4) other competent teachers and (5) those who would learn from these teachers. (By the way, don't let the word "teachers" throw you off; Paul is talking about everyday people like *you* teaching what you know to another person.)

Become a Barnabas

A good example for Timothy and the rest of us to follow would be that of Barnabas and Paul. We first meet Barnabas in Jerusalem where he donated some real estate profits to the poverty-stricken church. Later, we find him trusting Paul when the Jerusalem elders did not. After that he recruits Paul as a leader in the Antioch Church (another trust issue). Then he *leads* Paul out on their first missionary journey—Barnabas's name is always mentioned first in those verses, suggesting that he was the leader. Finally, he gives way to Paul as the leader since Paul apparently grows to become the stronger leader in their relationship as his name is written first whenever the two are mentioned in later passages.

This must have blessed Barnabas. To have your disciple surpass you is the greatest gift you can receive as a disciplemaker. Unfortunately, Barnabas and Paul's relationship didn't end well (some of yours won't either) when they got mad at each other and parted company at the beginning of a second missionary trip for each of them. This separating of the ways was over the presence of John Mark on their ministry team. Paul wouldn't forgive Mark for deserting them on their first trip, while Barnabas, the encourager, continued to bet on John Mark just as he had bet on Paul. Paul had surpassed Barnabas as a preacher, but he simply had not yet matured in the area of giving grace.

Paul withheld from John Mark the grace Barnabas had shown Paul and would continue to show Mark. After the breakup, Paul moved on to disciple Silas and Timothy while Barnabas went off with the wayward disciple, John Mark. By the way, Barney didn't fare too badly with either Paul or Mark. Paul wrote two-thirds of the books in the New Testament, and Mark wrote the first gospel—the one that stimulated Matthew, Luke and John to write theirs. You have to think that if it had not been for Barnabas's disciplemaking efforts, you might not be reading the book you hold in your hands.

I'd say Barnabas was a world-class disciplemaker. I believe this is true because he actually *did* what Jesus had commanded when He said to make disciples of all nations. But, Paul learned the disciplemaking process from Barnabas. If Barnabas had worked only with Paul, and none other, his life would still be a strong accomplishment for a guy never even mentioned in Scripture after he parts company with Paul.

By the way, after many years and many bruises, Paul would call for Mark to join him: "Get Mark and bring him with you, for he is useful to me for ministry" (2 Tim 4:11-12, *NKJV*). I think this is humorous, and it shows courage for Paul to have written those words after his earlier fallout with Barnabas over Mark. He swallowed some pride when he asked for Mark. Paul really had learned to manifest the grace he so majestically writes about in Romans and Galatians.

BUT *HOW* DO YOU MAKE DISCIPLES?

This part is pretty simple. You hang out with other people, intentionally bringing Jesus into your conversations. Your goal is to approximate *your* relationship with God in the life of the person you are discipling. It's all about spending time together with intent. I know I keep repeating this; now I want to explain it a little more fully.

I once had an interesting experience. The husband of one of my Christian friends was an avowed atheist. He was brilliant but a hard man to get along with. His rough exterior affected his marriage and it also ruined a few friendships in the local community.

After years of praying for this guy, he one day phoned me out of the blue. He said he had some questions about Christianity and wanted to talk. So, we agreed to meet for breakfast the following week. As it happened, I was rereading *Mere Christianity* by C. S. Lewis at the time. That book would figure strongly in our time together.

The guy showed up in the restaurant with two typed pages of questions about God. I was totally freaked out by his intellect and even more by his intimidating list of questions. This was one terribly bright atheist, and I'm not such a hot personal evangelist. I watched in terror as he scrolled down his list looking for an appropriate topic for the day's discussion.

Then I was amazed. The question he asked required only that I mimic C. S. Lewis's words from *Mere Christianity* that I had read the night before. We spent an hour talking about his question and its implications. My answer satisfied him. But he was fundamentally blown away when I revealed how I had come to that answer so easily. He left the restaurant believing that God had set up our conversation. That didn't make him into a Christ-follower, but it certainly got his attention.

And the story gets better . . .

The following Tuesday, the same thing happened. He got out his list and I popped off a satisfying answer to his difficult question. I then revealed that I had read the answer in *Mere Christianity* the night before. He bought a copy of the book that day, showed up in church the next week and accepted the Lord. He is walking strong to this day.

My conclusion: I am just a bit player in God's great drama. I don't need to do much but get out of bed in the morning with a heart toward disciplemaking. By the way, that man and I continued meeting on Tuesday mornings for several months. We answered a few more questions, but mostly he wanted to discuss his changed attitudes and work on making restitution for old sins. Our friendship is one of the high points of my life.

Discipling Those Not Yet Following Christ

The disciplemaking process starts before someone chooses to walk with the Lord. To accomplish this part of the journey, you must hang out with pre-Christians. If you only spend time with Christ-followers, a fair-sized part of your personal circle of concern will remain hell-bound.

A lady in our congregation recently told me an interesting story about her workplace. She was talking to a Bible prophecy guy who told her that, because the Lord is coming back so soon, we all need to avoid worldly contacts. By this he meant we should stay away from people who do not follow Jesus Christ.

Being somewhat new in her faith, she actually started to believe what this monkey told her. Then she remembered another friend. This woman is deeply into New Age philosophy, but she had recently confessed that she was praying to Jesus as a result of the time she spent with the lady from our church. My friend told me that she has decided that rather than avoid worldly contacts she wants to be found hanging out with non-believers when that final trumpet sounds. She may have a gift for evangelism, or perhaps she simply gets the idea of disciple-making better than most.

If the person is not yet a Christ-follower, you obviously wouldn't center everything in your relationship around the Lord. You find subtle ways of bringing God onto the table. Perhaps you tell of a miracle that happened through prayer. You let your jewelry, the books you are reading and personal experiences become conversation starters. This process allows you to announce your faith in God without preaching it. If your friend has problems, you respectfully offer to pray. You might even ask them to pray for you. Everyone prays, and people are honored when you ask for their prayer.

Just be sure the circumstances tilt toward the relational aspects of living your faith. Don't fall into the trap of overdoing the intellectual side of your walk with God.

Discipling Newly Minted Christians

We use the *Alpha Course,* which presents the basics of the Christian faith, to a great extent in our church. It is a practical example of relational disciplemaking. We eat dinner together for half an hour, and then we watch a half-hour video. Finally, we spend another 45 minutes to an hour collecting everyone's opinion about what we heard on the video. After meeting for a few weeks, the groups begin to engage in prayer—serious need-meeting prayer. All told, the relational stuff takes 75 minutes versus 30 minutes of intellectual input. We are helping move people toward Christ through friendly relationships.

I'm not selling Alpha, here. Any such system can be a starting point for discipling new followers of Christ. You just need to be sure you have such a system in place. And it doesn't need to be a church program—you can start something on your own with a couple of friends.

I'm always surprised when I hear people say things like, "My church is too small to do anything like Alpha," when, in fact, these tools seem to work better with smaller groups than with larger ones. Alpha works so well with small groups that we've purchased lending copies of the DVDs to aid our church members who want to host Alpha groups in their homes or in conference rooms in the marketplace. One guy from our congregation even hosted an Alpha group with his shipmates while they patrolled the Pacific on deployment with the U. S. Navy.

Balance Intellectual and Relational Aspects

You and I must resist the temptation toward pride that comes with too much knowledge. Paul warned of this: "But while knowledge makes us feel important, it is love that strengthens the church" (1 Cor. 8:1).

Scripture is clearly warning against prioritizing knowledge above relationships. Yet, we see so many disciplemaking programs that aim to do that very thing. You can see the results of them in local churches where knowledge without love makes for a pretty dead experience. Worse yet, go on the Internet and read the rantings of some of the self-appointed theologians who populate cyberspace. Is it any wonder that the Church isn't growing in America?

We must focus on the *relational* aspect of disciplemaking because that is what actually strengthens this wonderful thing we call church. If you notice the list of activities describing the prototype church in Acts 2, the word "fellowship" immediately follows the "apostle's teaching." Even prayer comes later in the list (see v. 42). I think that healthy, loving prayers issue from good, honest fellowship or intentional relationships.

Remember, Jesus was speaking of relationships when He said, "If two of you agree here on earth concerning anything you ask, my Father in heaven will do it for you. For where two or three gather together as my followers, I am there among them" (Matt. 18:19-20). When we hang out together in His name, He shows up to enjoy the fellowship—and it is then that prayer becomes powerful.

Fellowship always counts. When disciplemaking is relational, it remains healthy. When it substitutes anything else for relationship, the people involved become less than the Church.

Engage Intentional Wandering

I've never been in a healthy disciplemaking relationship that didn't involve getting off the point of whatever we were discussing. Actually, getting off the point may be the *real point*. And this is where much of what gets labeled as disciplemaking misses the boat.

Real life is messy. It is filled with more questions than answers. And humans need love more than any other commodity. Hence, conversational side streets and blind alleys become very important to the disciplemaking process.

I like to build disciplemaking relationships around pre-agreed upon content—we usually read a book and come together to discuss what we've read. In our home groups, or "mini-churches," we substitute the weekend sermon for the book. But our most fruitful conversations are usually those where a few words from the book or sermon trigger a thought that takes us away from the material we've chosen.

When strolling down these back alleys of discussion, people talk personally or ask about the things they really need to know. I live for these messy moments because they are often the growth points in a person's life. The place where life gets fun is in the midst of loving, listening relationship.

If you intend to become adept at disciplemaking, be sure you keep things loose enough for the conversation to go where it *needs* to go rather than just where you thought it should. Learn to listen to the conversation just below the surface of the actual conversation. Ask questions about that and you will learn much about the person you attempt to disciple.

Be Sure to Tell Stories

"Once upon a time" is a better teacher than "thou shalt not." You've got to watch this one closely because we humans are so prone to rules and religion. It is so very easy to get excited about helping another person only to find yourself burdening him or her with rules disguised as helpful hints.

How many times have you been put off by someone who crowded you to do something? He or she may have had the best intentions in the world but only succeeded in making you feel uncomfortable. Or he or she might even have backed you into a corner so tightly that you agreed to do something that felt unnatural enough that you walked away from the friendship.

Stories work—that's why Jesus told them so freely. It is always easier for people to "snatch and grab" truth when it comes packaged in the form of a story. Especially nice are true stories from your own life or from another person's God stories.

If there isn't a true story that makes your point, you can always make up a story. That's fair—Jesus' parables were stories He constructed in order to make a point. And His made-up stories are enduring. They've lasted for 2,000 years and are much easier to grasp than the moral codes of Moses.

A simple metaphor can work wonders. But you need to be careful that the hearer is familiar with the metaphor. The other day I heard a guy compare a fast-growing church to a bamboo forest—anyone who has tried to root bamboo out of his or her yard knows what a nice thing he was saying. But those who live in climates where bamboo doesn't grow would be lost in the forest he described.

However, "a heart melting like ice on a hot summer sidewalk" works well for just about anybody; or, "Good people will prosper like palm trees . . . virile still in old age" (Ps. 92:14, *THE MESSAGE*). Learning seems to be all about word-pictures.

Ensure Plenty of Ministry Time

Healthy discipling relationships include ministry time. By this, I mean honest, open conversations that shed light on real-life issues.

Sometimes things get resolved just by exposing them to the light of open conversation. More often, resolution comes when you agree in prayer. I can't imagine disciplemaking without prayer being central to the time spent together. Quite simply, you teach your disciples to pray. Let them discover that God answers their prayers as well as your own.

I remember one mini-church that included a man who had been estranged from his adult children for 22 years. He happened to mention it offhandedly one night in our disciplemaking group as we were breaking up to go home. He didn't ask for prayer, just said he wished he could one day see his boys. In fact, at that stage of his development, he would hardly pray about anything. He said God had more important problems than his, so he refused to bother Him.

One woman picked up on what he said about his boys and suggested that we should pray about God restoring this man's relationships with his sons. He didn't object, so we laid down our jackets and Bibles and prayed over his situation. He had last seen his older son when the boy was two years old. The younger son wasn't yet born when the marriage broke up. So this would be a strong miracle if it happened.

The very cool thing is that we prayed on a Wednesday, and the following Sunday this man received a call from California. It was his oldest son wanting to talk (remember, they hadn't spoken in 22 years). On Monday, our friend flew to the mainland to visit his son and was back in Hawaii in time to join us in our disciplemaking group by Wednesday evening.

Amidst all the rejoicing we discovered that the younger son still refused to have anything to do with his father. We prayed again, this time that God would soften the heart of the younger son. You guessed it . . . the following Sunday, the older brother called again to say, "Dad, would you be willing to talk with my brother?"

They got on the phone, and the next day this awestruck father was overjoyed to fly to the mainland for the second time in a week. Today the extended family is doing great. The man's current wife has even become friends with his ex-wife. Each family member is now following Jesus Christ.

The lessons I took from this drama is that God is willing to meet people like the woman who stopped us to pray—people who are serious about relational disciplemaking, and that answered prayer is born of openhearted fellowship.

Read and Practice

I spend lots of time discipling people toward ministry by using a method I learned while working on cars.

For a time in my life, I really got into restoring cars. I worked with a couple of antiques, but the core of what I did was to repair slightly aging Porches, Mercedes and Jaguars. I started out on a Mustang muscle car—the project took an eternity due to my lack of experience. Then I met a guy in our church who did the same kind of restoration work but on very expensive cars. There were Ferraris and Lamborghinis in his garage. My eyes nearly popped out of my head when I first visited his place.

This man discipled me in the art of auto bodywork and automotive restoration. Here's how he did it. First he gave me a book to read. After reading it and asking questions of him, we got together in his shop and he showed me how to do what I had read. He let me try some of the new tricks while he watched and coached me. Finally, he advised me to buy a couple of clunker cars off the street to practice on. By working on the low-end cars, I could learn from the book, from his supervision and from hands-on experiments where I couldn't do too much damage. The goal was to learn auto repair, flip the cars and make a little money while I was shooting for the abilities that would allow me to do the real thing.

I had been a pastor for at least 10 years before I met this man, but I have to say that I learned much about how to make disciples from this car restoration expert. I had somehow missed the *hands-on* part of the process—even when I read about it in the Bible and although I already had lots of experience with disciplemaking over the years.

For some reason, it didn't hit me that book learning and spending time together were not enough. There needs to be an element of "doing" for disciplemaking to really function well. We all require a faithful friend and some intellectual input plus an outlet to *practice* what we are learning. Once I got this down, I began trying as best as I could to do what I thought Jesus would do in my situation.

Today it works this way: If we are training someone for ministry, we begin by reading books in concert or, as mentioned earlier, we build the time around the weekend sermon. It is important that my disciples mark the book as they read it, highlighting whatever words or ideas the Holy Spirit used to speak into their hearts.

Then we come together to discuss what we underlined or wrote on the sermon notes. But the primary question is always the same: "What did the Holy Spirit say to you through this material?" As you can imagine, we run down lots of rabbit trails. Sometimes, in 90 minutes together, we'll actually spend less than 10 minutes on the study material and the rest of the time discussing real life as it intersects with what we've read.

Finally, there is homework beyond the book. This is the hands-on part of the process. We challenge each other to live out what we are learning—to live it out in our relationships with other people. If we are learning to pray with others, we seek opportunities to practice. If we are discussing spiritual gifts, we look for unobtrusive ways to implement them. If we are studying about money management, we hold our own personal finances up to what we are learning. We look for opportunities to teach others what we are learning. And we ask each other questions about how our efforts are coming along— there is an element of accountability in disciplemaking.

The disciples become disciplers. This is where the practice becomes a function of the learning process. Each disciple ought to be able to relate how his or her life lessons are working out in the lives of his or her own disciples. Practicing what we learn helps us to really learn it.

Teach Them to Journal

People have always kept diaries—at least some people. I never did until a few years ago. My journaling experiences are the product of a friend and the strong ministry he has built by teaching his disciples to journal. He's learned to outsource a lot of the work of the local church by building this powerful personal discipline into the lives of most of the people he leads. As a result of following his example, I now encourage everyone I disciple to do the same.

In journaling, I am able to capture promises that I believe God speaks to me, personally, from the Bible. I document my stronger needs as written prayers, dating both the first day I prayed and the date the answer arrived. I even jot down investment plans or ideas I might have for building stuff around our house.

As a person who never before kept a journal, I used to think of diaries and journals as belonging to adolescent girls. Journaling just wasn't a man-thing to do, in my mind. But now I can't live without journaling. Lots of the ideas for this book first appeared as scribbles in my journal. And with the advent of the smart-phone I've found an entirely new tool for journaling along with the opportunity to carry my journal everywhere I go.

As journaling has grown in importance in my life it became natural for me to introduce it to my disciples. I've noticed a stronger spiritual growth factor in those who journal that is distinct from those who do not.

Now, before I begin to sound cultish about this journaling process, let me make a couple of things clear. Nowhere in the Bible is journaling encouraged. It simply isn't to be found. However, the Bible clearly encourages us to *meditate* on God's Word.

Meditating isn't journaling. But you can't do much journaling of spiritual insights without first meditating on God's Word. So journaling becomes a tool to help disciples gain the fruitful ground of meditation.

The first Psalm describes the person whose "delight is in the law of the LORD, and in His law he meditates day and night. He shall be like a tree planted by the rivers of water, that brings forth its fruit in its season, whose leaf also shall not wither; and whatever he does shall prosper" (Ps. 1:2-3, *NKJV*).

I don't know about you, but I really like that idea about everything I attempt growing to prosperity. For that reason, meditating on Scripture and journaling my thoughts are now strong factors in my life and in the lives of those I disciple.

Walk Your Talk

I travel a lot and most of my travels take me overseas. I've been in some pretty crazy places in mostly developing nations. But my most fearful journeys have been to Europe.

Twice I traveled all the way from Hawaii to Europe only to find no one at the airport to pick me up. The first time was when I arrived in Brussels, Belgium, and waited two hours before finally making contact with someone who was able to give me a progress report on my ride from the airport. It seems that an accident in a tunnel in Holland had stranded my ride from Brussels for several hours. Of course, my anxiety level dropped with that knowledge and everything eventually worked out the way it should.

The second time was worse. I came through customs in Lisbon, Portugal, and found no one there to pick me up. For an hour I kept circling the customs exit, pretending that I had just arrived. I hoped to discover a person in the crowd holding my photo while looking for my face. But it was a no-go. Finally, I searched my briefcase for a local phone number only to discover that I didn't have one (which comes from being too dependent on others to make travel arrangements). Then I phoned back to Hawaii only to discover that our office was closed for a holiday.

Eventually, I connected with one of our staff members at their home. It was the person who had made arrangements for the trip. She had a local number for the church I was working with in Lisbon. But when I phoned that number it turned out to be the phone number for the nursery school where the Lisbon church rented an office. I spoke with a woman at the school who informed me that this wasn't the right number for the church. She also said her own office was about to close for the day and started to say good-bye. I really freaked out when she attempted to end our conversation.

This lady was the only person I knew in Portugal (for about 40 seconds) and she was about to hang up, leaving me as helpless as I had ever been. I begged her to help me contact the people who had invited me to speak.

Twenty minutes later she called my phone booth to tell me that my ride was now on the way. The event hosts had earlier waited for me for more than two hours in front of the customs exit. They finally gave up and left the airport at almost the exact time as my plane touched down. It seems that my office had given them misinformation about my itinerary.

Misinformation about an itinerary can get you into a lot of trouble. So can misleading someone with your life. I recently heard another airport story that illustrates this. A preacher got off a plane only to be stranded in front of customs just as I was. He waited for more than an hour before another man cautiously approached him. When asked why it took him so long to make contact, the driver said, "You don't look like your picture." It seems that the photo the man had was several years old and the guest speaker had changed in appearance in the meantime.

Here is my question: Do you look like your picture? As a Christ-follower, your picture should resemble that of the

Christ-followers presented in the book of Acts. Because of these earliest Christians, people were healed and others were freed from satanic influence. The people in the surrounding culture encountered the powerful Holy Spirit through their engagement with those saints. It is a series of these life-changing moments that compose the picture God hopes to paint of His followers. We can ensure that we look like our spiritual picture as we step into an experiential walk with God. We need to *practice* what we teach. And, of course, we need to find a way to build our own experiences with God into the lives of those we would attempt to make our disciples. If they know about God but don't experience Him, we've fallen short of our calling.

Build a Continuum

For a church to become a disciplemaking continuum, there needs to be a unified plan for making disciples. We've discovered a simple one.

We do this beginning with junior high mini-church leaders and progress through to adult mini-church leaders. As mentioned earlier, the only difference between this and our minichurches is that we read books together in leadership groups. While at the level of discipling masses of Christ-followers in small groups, we discuss the pastor's sermon from the previous weekend. All in all, we gather data, apply it to life and then support one another's life application through prayer and personal encouragement.

Now, there are ways to discuss material and there are ways you shouldn't. This surely is not a time for criticizing the pastor or an author's character. Nor is it a time for someone to regurgitate what the pastor, or the book, said. Re-preaching a message is a waste of everyone's time. Finally, it is not a time to build on the data by displaying our knowledge through further teaching. Our time together is all about relationship and ministry. It centers on material already gleaned and is heavy on application of God's word to our lives. It is also a time for communication with God through the Holy Spirit.

When I run either a leadership group or a mini-church, we start with food for about a half hour. I encourage people to bring leftovers because it lightens the financial burden of preparing food for the meeting. Besides that, leftovers always come with a story, and stories build relationships.

After fellowship and food, we each speak a word or two (I really mean just one or two words) that characterize what we remember of the sermon. This just gets the material off the mental hard drive and onto the desktop of our minds. Then we each answer this question, "What did the Holy Spirit say to you while the pastor was talking?" Leadership groups answer the same question, but the source material is whatever book we are reading.

This question is important because the Spirit speaks different things to different people—He has a way of bending words to fit His purposes. After sharing our insights, we discuss what we will do because of what the Spirit said, and we close by praying for each other in groups. We do prayer a little differently from a typical church group. We *never* take prayer requests; instead we restrict our prayers to issues brought up in the course of our earlier discussions. This "prayer boundary" helps us maintain focus on applying the Spirit's direction to the important issues in our lives. If it wasn't important enough to surface earlier in the evening, we will leave it to private prayer time. We want to use our time together to pray for life's more pressing needs. Along with the prayer comes the promise, "If I pray aloud for you in this meeting I am committing to pray for you for the next seven days."

The following week, while we are sharing food, we find ourselves asking, "What happened to you since we prayed for you?" You can be sure that our fellowship grows stronger as we share the results of those answered prayers. And the results of answered prayer are usually amazing. When people pray seriously for each other, love grows between them.

My wife likes to summarize disciplemaking efforts with the acronym RAP. It stands for Review, Apply and Pray. You review the material you have agreed to look at, you tell how it applies to your own life and then you pray for each other, asking God's help with the application. This is a very simple yet highly effective tool. This simple process is at the center of all our organized disciplemaking efforts. It has birthed more than 700 congregations in four decades.

Don't Forget OJT

The best way to learn something is to *do* it. When our kids were small, my wife and I always tried to enlist their "help" with any household project so they would become familiar with tools and unafraid to handle a task when they grew older.

The results showed up positively and negatively. There was the day when my four-year-old son completely took apart his tricycle, much to his mother's dismay. And there was the happy occasion when my wife and I came home to find our teenage daughter calmly adjusting the headlights on her car. (By the way, she got this rather difficult task right on the first attempt.)

My point is that both kids learned how to do things because we let them get their hands dirty. Sometimes the results were terrific, and sometimes they were less than desirable. But if you don't make a few messes you never really learn much about life. Today, both of our children are deeply involved in

ministry and have strong Christian families. We think it is because we kept them involved in ministry from a very early age.

This idea of on-the-job-training, or OJT, is not foreign to
our culture. It is how we teach some of our most complicated
skills. Flying airplanes, brain surgery and passing footballs in
the NFL are all taught and refined on the job.

Another story of OJT disciplemaking actually worked out
on two levels. One of my friends pastors a large church in
Kobe, Japan. He recently solicited volunteers to help remodel
an old house into a coffee shop that the church set up for outreach and disciplemaking.

One of the volunteers turned out to be an eight-year-old
half-Japanese–half-African boy. Anyone familiar with Japan
knows that this child is in a racially difficult position. It is difficult for people of foreign extraction to thrive in Japanese culture. Worse yet, his father has abandoned the family, leaving
the boy without a strong adult male role model to coach him
trough the treacherous waters of adolescence.

My friend immediately saw a disciplemaking opportunity
when he enlisted the boy in a relatively simple task on the construction job. A fellow staff member quickly upbraided the
pastor for putting the boy to work because he was so young.
He assumed that the boy would be a drag on the project.

The boy's task was simple for an adult but challenging to
him. He was to fill a large hole with concrete fragments from
the dismantling of a part of the building's foundation. The
hole would later be covered with concrete to form a new patio
for outdoor dining. This young boy's work would save the
church money by cutting back on the expense of extra concrete to fill in the hole.

After watching that little boy work hard for eight hours,
and after witnessing the instruction and voluminous praise

my friend showered on his young helper, the critic learned something. He saw my friend assume a fatherly role in the life of that young boy—one that he will maintain for many years. And he saw the pride the boy took in his work. You could say that both the boy and the critic were discipled via on-the-job-training that day. The boy learned something of his own value and gained a father figure. The church staffer learned that no one is too young to disciple.

On-the-job-training pays off when discipling people in their relationship with Christ. It is always useful to ask a person you are discipling to help you with any ministry tasks you undertake. If you lead a ministry, bring your disciple along to help. If you pray for someone going through deep water, invite your disciple to pray with you as well. We learn best by doing.

At this point, I should insert a warning: Don't burn out your disciples with too many projects. You will always have a few disciples who are up for anything. If you let them, these people will work themselves to a frazzle and then give up. I've noticed that few burnt-out people ever risk coming back into ministry. Regulate OJT or it will cost you dearly. Protect your disciple's time as well as your own.

This brings me to that wonderful invention of God called church. If you notice, the New Testament never tells us to plant churches, only to make disciples. But the apostles always seemed to organize their disciples into churches. Wherever Paul went he did four things: (1) He proclaimed the gospel message; (2) he made disciples; (3) he appointed elders from among his disciples (which suggests that he planted a church); and (4) later he wrote letters to coach those churches and their leaders (he didn't even have email), further proving that church planting was his modus operandi.

A good example of on-the-job-training is wrapped up in Paul's description of a church meeting: "Well, my brothers and sisters, let's summarize. When you meet together, one will sing, another will teach, another will tell some special revelation God has given, one will speak in tongues, and another will interpret what is said. But everything that is done must strengthen all of you" (1 Cor. 14:26).

Do you see the expectation that Paul put on the Corinthian Christians? He believed that every member there was a player.

His instructions regarding prophecy in 1 Corinthians 14 suggest he anticipated that mistakes would be made (see vv. 20-31). He made room for baby steps into ministry when he set up instructions for judging prophecies. Also, note that he never suggested that the church judge the prophets, only the prophecies. His instructions there simply called for a check-and-balance system that anticipated mistakes when you learn by doing.

There must be a place for OJT in your church, or it simply doesn't measure up to the New Testament standard.

Try to Disciple in Groups

I mentioned this earlier, but it is worth underscoring here. Discipling in groups is so simple that it almost goes without saying. More important, it is a better use of your time to make disciples in groups than it is to do it one-on-one. Jesus did it, and so did Paul.

However, there is always the exception to any rule. Barnabas apparently spent time one-on-one with Paul. Peter and John appear inseparable in the early chapters of Acts. I try to use groups but will also invest time one-on-one depending on the circumstances. I immediately try to bring a brand-new

Christ-follower into a group, and I always disciple up-and-coming leaders in groups. But when spending time with a peer, I prefer one-on-one.

Sometimes a person should get private attention because of some special skill set or because they are getting ready to launch a unique project. I try to spend a couple of hours a week with every church planter as we get them ready for the launch. After that, I grab every bit of time I can get with them in the busyness of the new church. Coaching before and after a launch is extremely important. Every situation is a little different, but I still mostly favor discipling in groups because of the restraints on my time.

I also try to limit my personal disciplemaking efforts to people who *are already doing ministry* in some meaningful way.

I do regularly host an Alpha group so that I can remain in touch with some of the newest Christ-followers in our congregation. However, all of my other disciplemaking efforts are with people already in leadership. This is a simple matter of scheduling my priorities. I coach my disciples and they coach theirs.

I even refuse to offer counseling with anyone outside of my discipleship circles. When people call our office for counseling, we refer them back to their mini-church or some other disciplemaking circle. As you may guess, some people don't want to participate in a group. If a person refuses to join a disciplemaking circle in our church, then we simply refer them to a local Christian counselor. They can either pay money for counsel or they can give their time to a group of people who will love them and minister to them in a very personal way. The group is able to lavish time and love on an individual in ways that a professional counselor can not.

A lot of my time goes into disciplemaking, and I disciple my staff as my first priority. To me that discipleship meeting is more important than sermon planning, preaching or church administration. I run an Alpha group of beginning Christians. I operate a weekly disciplemaking group of newly minted and wannabe pastors. And, I do meet with a single individual on a weekly basis, but that is because I, personally, need one-on-one friendship. To me these activities are the best use of my time—and time is the most important element in any human life.

My priorities demand that active involvement in ministry is the ticket into my life in any meaningful way. When people ask how to get involved in ministry, I usually tell them to join a mini-church or some other ministry and make themselves useful enough that they get invited onto the leadership team.

I hope you catch my heart here. I am not a hard man, but I am on a mission to win the world to Christ. I have limited time and want to spend it well.

This is pretty straightforward stuff. You love God and then you love people. But you love them with purpose. You make disciplemaking a priority—a priority that Jesus set when He said, "Go and make disciples of all the nations" (Matt 28:19).

If I have to describe my priorities, the list would look something like this:

1. My wife and family
2. My personal disciples
3. Writing and preaching the best sermons that I can (mass disciplemaking)
4. Managing the church and traveling around teaching others to multiply disciples and churches
5. Writing books like this one in hopes of planting seeds in the hearts of people I've never met

Did you notice the flow of priority here—that my disciples are more important to me than preaching? And that preaching is more important than administration or writing?

CHAPTER TEN

FISHING POOLS
ALL AROUND

Jesus called His disciples to "follow Me, and I will make you fishers of men" (Matt. 4:19, *NKJV*). This of course has implications for us. As followers of Jesus Christ, we automatically *inherit* the calling to "fish" for people. It is our job to bring others into a relationship with God through His Son. And it isn't a difficult task at all. It usually just involves looking around you and making friends with those toward whom you have an affinity.

Lots of churches talk about their larger outreach events as "fishing pools" for disciplemaking. The idea is that the church works hard to bring outsiders to an event where members strike up conversations that lead to relationships, and so on. You can see where this is going. The new person moves from the position of a relative stranger to the group, and perhaps to the Lord, into a circle of new friends where it is hoped that discipleship happens.

The problem with that approach is twofold. First it runs churches ragged providing enticing programs. This method often takes energy away from operations that might better equip close-in members through disciplemaking. The second difficulty is that most people naturally gravitate toward their friends, no matter what the nature of the event. While the Christ-followers are having a great time at a fun-filled fishing pool event, outsiders can remain just that—outsiders.

This happens too often. And in response to this problem, church leaders can get worried and browbeat their members into reaching out to the new people. When this occurs, church members never really get to enjoy the fellowship of their peers. Operating church-driven fishing pools requires a delicate balancing act and immense energy on everyone's part in order to provide any success at all.

However, large groups can (and do) make great "fishing pools" for disciplemakers. But we've found that this approach mostly works better outside the circle of church activities than in them.

Every church is a *missionary* church. Your national and local cultures are *foreign* to the kingdom of God. As in every missionary situation, the missionary needs to embrace and adopt the local culture in an attempt to make spiritual inroads.

If you operate in a foreign culture, you can't expect your neighbors to simply come to hear what you have to say to them. Nor can you expect them to immediately embrace your values. You and I need a missionary mindset that allows us to penetrate a world that is foreign to Christ's kingdom. It is on us to adapt to the world around us. Paul put this nicely when he said, "I have become all things to all men, that I might by all means save some" (1 Cor. 9:22, *NKJV*).

We need to go where the people we are trying to reach go and spend time on their turf. And we must maintain a nonjudgmental attitude while introducing them to the love and power of God. We cannot judge their value system. We need the patience to allow God to change their values from the inside out. Once a person knows God's *love* and *power* (through praying about problems and concerns), they are much more likely to want to know more about your views about God. It is after the hook is in the jaw that you begin to reel in the fish.

You do this as you slowly introduce your new friends to the values of the kingdom of God. Attempt to press values too early and you will be seen as an uptight Christian attacking the lifestyles of others. However, if you remain in relationship until the Holy Spirit transforms the person, you'll discover in him or her a deep hunger for the values and standards of the kingdom of God.

I know people who have developed intentional friendships that resulted in people coming to Christ in activities as different as surfing together, a golf tournament or joining others in a political campaign. In each situation the believer was on the lookout to be a fisher of men, and the larger group provided that person with a natural fishing pool. Work, school, sports teams, school projects and golf outings all function as ready-made fishing pools for the alert fisherman.

A FOUR-YEAR PROJECT

I started high school when I was 13. I weighed 115 pounds on my first day in that strange new world. The kid sitting next to me in my first class each morning topped the scales at 265. His size was intimidating but he was one of the friendliest people I've ever met.

In our freshman year, he played first-string varsity football as a defensive tackle—he was so good that he made all state, first team varsity at age 14. By the way, did I mention he was also the Oregon state varsity high school heavyweight-wrestling champion in his freshman year? He beat much older and more experienced kids with amazing regularity. My friend maintained both of these achievements for all four years of high school. I, meanwhile, remained a skinny and decidedly non-athletic runt.

But we became friends. We shared a locker in the hall during our freshman year. We joined the same after-school social clubs. He defended me from bullies. We got afternoon jobs in the same company. In short, we hung out together for four years.

Our friendship made high school better. It was a good friendship in every way. And, of course, we also got into mischief. During our senior year, we were given to calling our mothers from the school office to say we were coming home sick. Then we'd each use the phone in the hall to tell them that we were suddenly feeling better. Liberated from school, we'd sneak in a few extra hours and some extra bucks at work. On those days, we'd often walk the two miles from school to work to save the bus fare.

It was on one of those hikes to work that my friend accepted Christ. We'd talked about God from time to time, but on this day it just felt right to ask him if he'd like to invite Christ into his life. As we walked across a bridge over Portland's Willamette River, my buddy became a follower of Jesus Christ.

From that day on our relationship changed. My role became that of a coach or mentor. I'd been working at introducing him to the Lord for nearly four years before it finally came to fruition. He never joined my church. Our relationship, not organized religion, was the key to his initial growth in the Lord, and it took. He went on to live a strong Christian life.

This would be a good place to insert that I haven't always been so successful. I had an even closer friend during those high school days. This was another athlete who sat in front of me in nearly every class—a product of seating students alphabetically according to their last names. We ate lunch together nearly every day for four years. We worked hard in classes we liked (striving for an *A* or a *B*). At the same time, in classes we didn't like, we cheated (very hard) to get a *C* while doing as little normal study as possible. Our theory was that a lazy teacher deserved laziness from us, but I suspect we worked harder for those illicit *C*s than for the legitimate higher grades—crime doesn't pay.

But here is the rub: I never once shared my faith with him. Don't much know why, but I seemed intimidated in this particular part of our relationship. The news got a lot sadder after I moved to Los Angeles to attend college. My mom sent me a four-inch news clipping informing the world that my friend was killed in a car accident. This happened a year after we graduated. I still lament the one that I let get away.

My point here is that God presents us with fishing pool opportunities nearly every day of our lives. It is up to us to make the best of them. If you and your church can create a culture of outreach and disciplemaking, then the whole process begins to feel a lot more natural and less forced. Besides that, it really works.

SURF STORIES

My first pastorate was in a church in a Southern California beach town. Our congregation of young adults was mostly from the surf culture. They managed to penetrate their world with the gospel. Our guys seemed to just naturally talk about their faith while waiting for waves. Lots of surfers found their way into our disciplemaking network, and several went on to become pastors.

I fondly remember all the wet heads showing up on Sunday mornings after early morning surf sessions. But one event stands out above the rest. I remember a brand-new believer who came to church weeping one morning. As a pre-Christian, he had been a violent person. This became apparent one day when I met several of his friends at Venice Beach. Whenever we approached a group of his acquaintances, everyone would stop talking and greet him with more fear than respect.

Back to our story. This man was the disciple of one of our young surfers but had known the Lord for only a couple of weeks when someone cut him off on a wave one Sunday morning before church. He instinctively punched the guy, breaking his nose, while both competed for that small piece of water.

He later came to church weeping because he couldn't get the guy to accept Christ after breaking his nose. "I helped him out of the water, even helped him clean up the blood, but he wouldn't listen when I tried to tell him about Jesus." Not a pretty story, but it does show that disciplemaking is a process that requires patience with the newly born again.

We did well with surfers in Southern California, but when I moved to Hawaii, I saw our involvement with the surf culture escalate beyond my wildest dreams. One of our largest church services was born in a surfer's Bible study that met in a small home on Friday evenings.

One day, I went surfing with a bunch of our kids (they were literally half my age). They all stopped at the water's edge to pray for safety and a good time during that day's surf session. This short prayer time included both Christians and pre-Christians.

I had never seen anything like it. My peers and I probably prayed for the same things but we did so privately. For certain we didn't involve pre-Christians in our prayers. These young people set themselves up to be fishers of men through praying for a good time. Here is another case of using a larger group outside of the church and its programs as a fishing pool for introducing people to Christ. The prayer at the beach set everyone up for quite natural questions like, "Why did you do that?" Such questions lead to discussions that bring people to the Lord. This is disciplemaking in the fishing pool.

I've got lots of golf and fishing stories from church members, but I'll save them for another book.

WORKPLACE STRUGGLES

Two of my friends number among the nicest people I know. But they started out as enemies—not mortal enemies, but the kind of people who just strike each other wrong from day one.

Worse yet, they had to work very closely together. One is the CEO of the organization where they work. The other is a vice president. It is the CEO who was the Christ-follower. The workmate was not. After years of struggling over work, the one person prayed the other into a friendship and then a relationship with God through Jesus Christ.

Today they partner in important projects at our church. To drag out an overused phrase, they are pillars in our church. I think I take away as much support from those two as from any other people I know. I don't know how I would function as pastor if the one person hadn't seen the workplace as a fishing pool and viewed himself as a fisher of the other, even when the going wasn't so good.

A BEER WITH THE BOYS

A friend in Japan told me that he never really infiltrated the lives of the young men in the large church he helps pastor until he started going out for an occasional beer with several young men in the church.

Drinking is very much a part of Japanese male culture. When the pastor joined in, he soon found himself accepted in a different way than before. He also found himself answering a host of questions about God and the Bible. Putting aside whatever you think of alcohol, those young men have grown into spiritual leaders in that church. And this most certainly would not have happened if my friend hadn't gone out with them. In fact, after several years, one of those original young men is now a staff pastor in that congregation.

Then there is a friend of mine who goes out every couple of months with the same group of pre-Christian friends to sample fine wine along with exotic cheeses and breads. He's been doing this for years, always taking a lot of good-natured ribbing about his walk with God.

It recently paid off when one of his buddies ran into marital trouble. The guy phoned the *only* consistent Christian he knew to say, "My marriage is in trouble, and I need the Lord or

I'll be getting a divorce." Spending time with others pays off. We can easily identify the natural fishing pools all around us. We can succeed at evangelism by realizing that disciplemaking most often starts outside the four walls of a church building. It should be our everyday business.

MORE STRUCTURED DISCIPLEMAKING

Once someone makes a decision to follow Christ, your relationship with that person changes.

This is why I always ask people who prayed in church to accept Christ to tell someone they suspect is praying for them or might be preaching to them. I want them to tell that person within the first 24 hours of their decision because it automatically sets up that coaching relationship we call disciplemaking. I do this because disciplemaking seldom happens by accident. There often needs to be an institutional push to get it going. There is surely a place for planning, structure and intentionality about a church that decides to obey the Lord in this important area.

We started the chapter discussing fishing pools, or places where we can try our stuff at the task of fishing for men and women. The organized church events often work well, but we needn't wait for them in order to get to the job at hand. Picture your life as a marshland where you daily negotiate between these fishing pools or, as I referred to earlier, as circles of concern. There are people all around you with empty hearts who need what you have. The impetus belongs to you, *not* to your pastor. To mix metaphors, horribly, we fishers of men need to see the fields that Jesus said "are already white for harvest!" (John 4:35, *NKJV*).

While talking about fields that are ripe for harvest, or fishing pools waiting for willing fishermen, it might be wise to remember that Jesus anticipated that there would not be enough people willing to accomplish the task. This is why, after lamenting over the spiritual needs of outsiders, He told His disciples what to do about the problem. He said, "The harvest is great, but the workers are few. So pray to the Lord who is in charge of the harvest; ask him to send more workers into his fields" (Matt. 9:37-38).

Whenever I notice the task of disciplemaking waning in our congregation, I simply go to prayer to ask the Master for more labor. Call them harvesters or fishermen, we need more intentional disciplemakers, and it seems that all we have to do is ask.

CHAPTER ELEVEN

DON'T JUST STAND THERE, DO SOMETHING

A couple of years ago, I visited Sapporo, Japan, in the height of winter. I was impressed with snow plowed into mountains, half-again my height, at the side of the road. The snow was beautiful, and preparations for the annual Ice Festival were intriguing.

I was surprised to discover that the daily weather gets sunny and fairly warm, while returning to a deep freeze overnight. It seems that Sapporo gets fresh snow each morning, then just enough sun to make the snow soggy. Each night the temperature drops sufficiently to turn the soggy snow into a mass of ice. And it is here that our story begins . . .

Snowflakes drifting through the sky feel kind of friendly. They wrap the world in a blanket of loveliness, even hushing the harsher sounds of everyday life. It is easy for snow to lull you into inaction. And that is what happened to the owners of a couple of bicycles I found entombed in an icy snowbank.

These bikes were frozen in place—encased in a mound of ice that rose higher than their fenders. You couldn't get them out of the ice without breaking, melting or destroying them in some other way.

The owners had made a crucial mistake when the snows first appeared. Perhaps there had been a couple of days when the snow didn't stick. Or maybe they just got lazy. Either way, lethargy left their bikes useless while other cyclists regularly traversed the plowed roads as they went about their daily business.

But the fact that the bikes were covered in ice wasn't the only problem. They could also get lost forever. Snowplows regularly tossed the white stuff into high mounds, which were then bulldozed into parks or other off-road locations. A snow-covered bike, in a park, might eventually get plowed under a mountain of ice.

What's that got to do with you and me? Well, sometimes we get fresh new ideas—ideas that are so good they lull us to sleep. They seduce us into lethargy. Their very freshness is seductive. We find ourselves wrapped in a sweet blanket of innovation only to succumb to the wax and wane of cultural temperatures.

In short, our fresh ideas melt a little over time. If we're not careful they can freeze into institutional snowbanks. In fact, that may be happening to you as you read this book. You may "freeze" into inaction by intellectualizing and analyzing what you've read. You may hold back because of some fear of getting too involved or some other reason. You would still *own* the knowledge printed on these pages, but it wouldn't do anybody any good.

The problem with those Sapporo bike owners is that they settled for ownership rather than ridership. In an unholy mix of metaphors, they got off the pony and left it to freeze to death.

My concern is that you turn personal knowledge of Christ into action. Routine can lead to a kind of spiritual paralysis resembling the fate of those bikes. I think the key to success in disciplemaking is a preference for action over ownership. We must keep moving in order to keep from getting stuck in the icebank.

THAT CRUCIAL FIRST STEP

Have you noticed that organizations never do anything of themselves? It takes people within those organizations to act on ideas or nothing gets done.

The Bible says that when God called Abraham, he *moved* by faith, "It was by faith that Abraham obeyed when God called him to leave home and go to another land that God would give him as his inheritance. He went without knowing where he was going" (Heb. 11:8).

That Scripture seems an obvious statement, and not such a big deal, until you think on it a little longer. Abraham was very much alone among a bunch of idolaters. This included his father, since the Scriptures tell us that God commanded Abram (as he was then called) to leave his *father's* household and *his* idols. The term "idolater" probably included Abraham's wife and even his nephew, Lot, who would finally make the journey with him. Previous to the experience with God, Abraham may have been an idol worshiper who was interrupted by the surprise communication from heaven.

However you slice it, what God asked Abraham to do was to take a mammoth step into the unknown. He would leave behind everything familiar for a package of blessing only represented by a bunch of words—yet, he went!

Abraham could have just sat on his word from the Lord, rejoicing that God had spoken to him, as some do. He could have rationalized the word to mean that he should abandon idols and step into a deeper walk with God, again a mistake many make. Or, he could do what he did—make preparations to get out of Dodge.

I think Abe took the first step when he *decided* to obey the Lord. In other words, it was a step he took in his heart and mind. The second step would have been scarier, that of *informing* his wife of his plans. Without these two actions the rest would not be history and you wouldn't be reading this book. First steps count.

Because Abraham stepped into faith, he indeed became the father of a great nation, prospered materially and became a blessing to all the nations just as God had predicted. Likewise, if Paul and Barnabas hadn't said yes to the Holy Spirit

DON'T JUST STAND THERE, DO SOMETHING

during that prayer meeting in Antioch, the world would be a very different place today. Obedience requires action, but that action always starts with a simple decision to do whatever God asks of us.

A SUREFIRE WAY TO AVOID MISTAKES

What would you say if I promised you a secret that would guarantee you would never make another mistake in your entire life? You would probably think I was a nutcase (or maybe a genius). But it is true. I can teach you how to avoid all mistakes.

Avoiding mistakes is simple. Just never attempt anything difficult. Of course, while you are busy avoiding mistakes you might notice that you aren't accomplishing anything of any importance.

If you hope to make a difference in this life, you have to take risks. You must make mistakes on the road to accomplishment. A quarterback who never threw an interception never won a Super Bowl. The home-run kings of Major League Baseball have also consistently been the strikeout kings of the sport; by swinging for the fences, they score often, but they also miss a lot of pitches.

What does this have to do with making disciples? A lot!

Reading and talking about something are different from actually doing it. I have two good friends who are members of a large and historic Christian organization on our island. Their group has been in Hawaii for more than 100 years. Both men have wishfully asked about how they could build a disciplemaking continuum in their churches. One even came to visit some of our groups. Both stated that they intended to get something going.

However, several years have passed with no action from either of them. The reason? Fear! They are afraid of disturbing their overseers. From where I sit, I'd say their bikes are stuck in a snow bank.

If you call people to follow you while you follow Christ, you *will* suffer misunderstandings at some point. Some will follow only to fall away later. You'll get into some arguments and other Christians may even accuse you of building your own kingdom.

But worse of all, you will make some real mistakes. You may find yourself fresh out of answers when a pre-Christian asks an honest question about God and life. You may commit leadership blunders that cost you and your followers. You may explain something only to discover that you were wrong and need to correct yourself in front of your disciples. So what? At least you are doing something instead of sitting on your hands. So don't just stand there with the ball in your hands, disciple someone.

GOD'S VISION AND YOU

Apparently, God thinks the entire world can be brought into a relationship with His Son. Why else would Jesus state that since *all* authority has been given to Him, are we to go and make disciples of *all* nations?

I used to have problems with that Scripture. I thought it meant I was to try to make a few disciples in our town. My assumption was that if I did my small part someone else would fill in the blanks to reach the rest of the world. In fact, I was once guilty of teaching that "the day of missions" was past since the missionaries of the previous century had sowed seeds in virtually every country. I mistakenly thought that the people in other countries were now completely responsible to make disciples in their own countries without further help from the outside world.

Later, my vision stretched to where I thought that if we returned to missions, taking the gospel to every language group, it would hasten the return of the Lord. In other words, if we made a *few* disciples in each culture, we would usher in the kingdom of God. Talk about limited vision. I couldn't see that Jesus was actually talking about eating the whole enchilada—His words really meant what they said. We are to go to the ends of the earth making disciples of all nations. God is interested in individuals, but He is even more interested in entire people groups.

There is an ancient Mongolian proverb that says, "You can't measure the sky with your window and you can't measure the ocean with your bucket." I would add, "You can't measure God's call by your own vision." When I finally stopped trying to measure God's call by my limited vision, I found the possibilities unlimited.

As a young man, my idea of God's call on my life was to plant a small church and raise up a disciple. I would then send him away for theological training. After that our church could bring that disciple back to take my place. At this point, I would become free to move to another town and plant another church. I thought I could accomplish this routine between five to seven times during my lifetime.

I also thought that the churches I could plant would all be congregations numbering under 50 people. So, five or seven small churches would become a way to leverage my limited gifts. Do you see how limiting our own vision for our lives can be?

My plan seemed reasonable since I am (still) a soft-spoken person without the kind of charisma we so often associate with effective leaders. But, God had a better idea. In my first pastorate, I discovered that I could lead several disciplemaking groups at a time and that I could infuse those disciples with a desire to *reproduce* what they had.

Eventually, one guy turned a single disciplemaking group into a church, and we caught the bug of church multiplication. We began turning disciplemaking groups into churches and grew into a movement. We learned that a disciplemaking group is infinitely reproducible and that a disciplemaking continuum is virtually unstoppable. That's why we have stuff brewing on every continent today. It's also why our congregation is home to vibrant young people eager to multiply the Church in places we've never been.

But what does my own story have to do with you? Well, we're back to Abraham. No one ever gets anywhere without that simple step of saying yes to whatever God is saying. This is true even if you can't yet envision the entire picture.

Don't know whom to call to follow you? Don't sweat it. Just tell God that you will call whomever He indicates you should call.

Fearful of doing it all wrong? Then simply count on making a few mistakes. You'll get over it. After all, you learned to walk by falling down. You hung onto furniture till your fat little fingers could support you no more and you went sprawling on the floor. I promise you that you will make your share of mistakes. But we learn more through our mistakes than through our successes. So reject guilt or shame over mistakes, and get moving.

TEST, TEST, TEST . . .

Whenever anyone in my circle comes up with a promising but scary idea, we decide to test it. By that I mean that we don't jump in with both feet, we just stick a toe in the water. After all these years, we are still a little unsure of our own vision: "Is this a *God* idea, or just another *good* idea?"

We set ourselves up for either a small success or a small failure by taking baby steps into whatever idea presents itself. The cool thing is how often our small steps result in large successes. This is the wisdom you get from people who find success in the stock market. They take baby steps when buying into a position in the market. That way they can watch for growth or failure without taking great risk. The important thing is to limit risk so that you can get something up and running. You'll never really know if an idea is from God unless you try it on for size.

Please don't allow the last few paragraphs to get your mind wandering toward large projects. We're still talking about calling someone to "follow me, as I follow Christ." Taking that first step to call someone to walk with you into disciplemaking also opens the door to God's leading and provision. You agree to do it, but only as the Lord leads and provides whatever you need to accomplish the goal. If there is something lacking, you can be sure He will provide it, but only after you say yes to whatever He asks.

BELIEVING OTHERWISE

I can remember a book that shaped my thinking while I was still in high school. It was the biography of Roger Bannister, the first man to run a four-minute mile. It was previously thought that no man could ever run that fast. Bannister believed otherwise. And he broke the barrier. The funny thing is that within months several others surpassed the same unbreakable barrier. Today, hot high school athletes routinely run a mile in less than four minutes.

The upshot of all this is that most barriers exist only in the minds of those who believe in them. What we believe influences our behavior, not the other way around. If you decide that God could use you to make disciples, you will find that you can do it—over and over again.

But I promise you that you will have to deal with mistakes along the way. Bannister didn't just go out and break an unbreakable record. He lost races along the way—probably fell a time or two. If we fear making mistakes or looking foolish, we can't expect very much. If we can push through whatever freezes us in place, we can expect victory in our own lives as well as in the lives of other people.

Remember those two frozen bicycles? They got stuck because of benign neglect. If the owners had merely kept using them, the snows never would have trapped them into a state of uselessness. It is the same with us, really. All we need to do is grab onto the opportunities around us to be successful in the business of God's kingdom.

CHAPTER TWELVE

WHO SHOULD
DISCIPLE ME?

I can't say that anyone ever actively discipled me. I've had some very good mentors but no one who *intentionally* spent regular time in disciplemaking.

My mentors include a lady I met at a summer camp as an 11-year-old boy. She had great input in my life and I know her well to this day. But as a single woman, she was never in a position to disciple me up close, especially as I grew older.

I worked with a pastor for seven years who shaped me in many strong ways. He shared wonderful insights into ministry, but in those days and in our movement there was no thought of intentional, ongoing disciplemaking. He gave me much but would have given me more if disciplemaking had been a part of our church culture.

It is this lack of disciplemaking in most church cultures that holds many, if not most, from reaching full potential. A friend once told me that somewhere near 95 percent of students who enter seminary will not be in paid ministry two years after their class graduates. My own informal polling makes me believe this to be true. The reasons are probably many, including some who enter seminary without the gifting required for pastoral ministry. But, I have to think that some of this dropout rate is due to seminary graduates being thrust into ministry without someone to champion and disciple them in the finer points of working with church problems and the like. We need coaching for would-be leaders. This is coaching that reaches into lives well beyond the reach of a classroom experience.

I spent last evening discussing disciplemaking with a graduate of one of the finest seminaries in our nation. He told me that all he ever wanted was to disciple young people—he had wanted to remain a youth pastor all his life. Now in mid-life, he has served as a youth pastor, a missionary, a local church missions director and, finally, as a church planter.

The church he planted does not meet his expectations. It isn't growing. My advice was for him to pull together a few young people already in his church and disciple them personally. In other words, go back to being a youth pastor on Fridays while keeping the adult congregation happy the rest of the week.

My new friend immediately liked the idea but spent the next few hours struggling with how much it would differ from all he was taught in seminary. Now, this is an extremely bright man with an education far superior to mine, but he can't quite get to where he wants to go. I believe it is because no one has ever discipled him in a way that he can reasonably *imitate*. He knows a lot of good stuff, but no one ever truly coached him into ministry. There is great wisdom in Paul's words, "You should imitate me, just as I imitate Christ" (1 Cor. 11:1). The problem is you first need someone to imitate.

Sadly, the church has become so business-oriented and program driven that few pastors see themselves as chief equippers (can you tell by now that I believe pastors are *obligated* to disciple their staff members?). Because senior pastors usually set the cultural parameters of a church, many churches simply lack a disciplemaking mentality. Disciplemaking is not a part of their collective DNA, though it is central to the Great Commission. If this is the case in the church you attend, you may need to aggressively hunt for someone to disciple you.

SO, WHO SHOULD DISCIPLE YOU?

Let's start with some questions. Who brought you into a relationship with Christ? Who are the people in your circle that are farther along in their walk with Christ, or in ministry, than you? Who do you answer to in your particular ministry team? Finally, when all else fails, who is simply willing to disciple you?

MAKING **DISCIPLES**

Who Brought Me to Christ?

The person who helped you find a relationship with Jesus Christ is the prime candidate to disciple you. If he or she doesn't offer help, go ask for it. He or she will probably feel flattered that you did.

Who Is Farther Along?

If you are looking for someone to disciple you, perhaps you just need to look around for someone you like and respect who is also further along in his or her relationship with God than you are.

Simply ask that person if he or she would be willing to share an hour or so a week with you, discussing your growth in the Lord. A great place to begin is in any organized small group in your church, or perhaps a campus ministry if you are still in school.

The person may be too busy but able to help you find someone else to disciple you. This often happens to me—people hear me talk about disciplemaking and ask for access to my life. I either fit them into one of the groups I lead or I network them into a relationship with someone else.

What I am trying to say is that it is fair to ask . . .

Who Do I Answer to?

If you are serving the Lord in a local church or some other ministry, there is bound to be a person overseeing your efforts. That person *should* disciple you in that ministry *and* in your relationship with the Lord.

I know some churches where ministry teams are seen as disciplemaking groups. These people tend to grow strong in the Lord and usually progress to bigger ministry as time passxes. But, I've seen others who give only lip service to the

160   RALPH MOORE

idea of the ministry team as a disciplemaking group. New people learn the ropes in terms of their ministry tasks, but they don't get any discipling in terms of their personal life and relationship with Jesus Christ. In those situations, people are constantly burning out and needing replacement.

If you are serving someone, you have a right to ask him or her to schedule time to disciple you in your life with God. Doing so will not only enhance your life but also enhance that person's life.

Who Is Willing?

This person may not have been discipled himself, or herself, but if he or she is interested in you as a person and willing, grab on to that person. I think of Moses-Joshua, Elijah-Elisha and Barnabas-Saul in these terms. In each of these examples there is no evidence that the "older brother" was discipled by anyone. Yet, somehow he saw the value in making disciples.

You might simply approach someone who is busy discipling others. I find that people who make disciples are usually able to squeeze in one more person or adjust their schedules to fit around one more life. Either way, if a person understands the process and is willing to sacrifice time, he or she is a likely candidate. Ask the person to help you grow in your relationship with God as well as your personal ministry to others.

THE PRICE OF DISCIPLEMAKING

Remember this: If someone does give of himself or herself to disciple you, you are called to pass along the favor. A willingness to pass along what you receive is the price of admission.

We've looked at this Scripture several times in this book, but please think on it again. Paul wrote to his disciple Timothy, "Be strong through the grace that God gives you in Christ

Jesus. You have heard me teach things that have been confirmed by many reliable witnesses. Now teach these truths to other trustworthy people who will be able to pass them on to others" (2 Tim. 2:1-2).

The first part of the instruction is for disciples to attend to their own personal strengths, which come through the grace God gives. After that, one who has received instruction is to pass it along to others. But more than just passing it along, that person is *responsible* to see that his or her disciples make disciples.

I just finished teaching for a couple of days in a Bible school located in Singapore. One student is the pastor of more than 400 high school students. He told me that his pattern for disciplemaking is built around four questions:

1. How are you doing?
2. What is God showing you in the Bible?
3. What are you going to do about what God has shown you?
4. How are your disciples doing in their ministry to others?

I get the feeling this young man understood what Paul was getting at.

Paul then goes on to describe the suffering that comes to faithful followers of Christ. This may simply involve the cost of giving away time when you could be doing something else. Or, it may involve persecution.

I recently visited a country where believers live under constant surveillance from the government, and I met one family who had been evicted from their home (and city) seven times for converting others to Christ. The result of that gov-

ernment interference is that they have now planted seven ille-
gal churches. Had they been left alone they would have stuck
with just the first one. That government is actually responsible for the multiplication of a single church into seven of
them. Persecution may be personally painful, but it often produces magnificent results in God's kingdom.

After dealing with the toughest part of being a disciplemaker, Paul admonished Timothy about his priorities. He
wrote, "Soldiers don't get tied up in the affairs of civilian life,
for then they cannot please the officer who enlisted them.
And athletes cannot win the prize unless they follow the
rules" (2 Tim. 2:4-5).

This brings to mind Jesus' statement, "When someone has
been given much, much will be required in return; and when
someone has been entrusted with much, even more will be required" (Luke 12:48). If someone disciples you, you should
make discipling others one of your life's higher priorities.

Paul's message to Timothy wasn't only about the price you
pay to serve. He also described its joys. He wrote, "Hardwork-
ing farmers should be the first to enjoy the fruit of their
labor" (2 Tim. 2:6). There are rewards for faithful disciplemaking. The chief reward is to watch someone succeed in life who
might otherwise have been destroyed by the world and its
machinations. Paul was so into the reward factor that he could
write, "I am willing to endure anything if it will bring salvation and eternal glory in Christ Jesus to those God has chosen" (2 Tim. 2:10).

A healthy church will reflect the same values as Paul describes in these verses. The pastor functions as the chief equip-
per, directly discipling a group of people who in turn disciple
others who pass on what they are learning to others. I believe
that a pastor should actively and intentionally disciple his staff

while expecting them to disciple others. This absolutely *defines* the core of a disciplemaking continuum.

All of this happens apart from the traditional church matrix of programs and classes—we are talking about a disciplemaking continuum as the *chief* structural element in a local church. If a pastor makes disciplemaking a chief priority, it then follows that a healthy Christ-follower will do the same. So here are your prospects: Find someone to disciple you, even if you need to change churches to do it. And you may find that your church is so wrapped up in busyness that you will need to relocate to a different congregation just to find someone willing to disciple you.

When you've found a discipler, stick with him or her. After that (while you are still someone's disciple), pass the favor along to others who will pass it on again.

CHAPTER THIRTEEN

WHAT DO I OWE
MY TEACHER?

On a recent trip overseas, I had the opportunity to hear one of my disciples speak about what a disciple owes his teacher.

It was a heartwarming experience for me. He spoke in a church pastored by one of my former disciples, a man who has planted multiple churches and is a person I deeply respect. The message was meant for the members of that church and especially targeted those being discipled into leadership in that growing congregation. But the person most blessed by the teaching was myself.

This younger man described the blessings he sees Timothy returning to Paul. You could think of them as returns on investment in much the same way you may think of returns in the stock market. Of course there is the return that you see in the growth of the ministry. I think of that as the kind of return a stock gives as the price goes higher. But there are also the returns brought by dividends returned to the shareholder. In disciplemaking, relational returns resemble those dividends to me.

In all, the message was about five things a disciple should return to the person who is the principle teacher in his or her life. Each is a strong source of encouragement to anyone who has ever invested his or her life in making a disciple.

BE LOYAL

The first dividend is personal loyalty. I think it is important to understand that Timothy, by this time, could be considered as much a missionary as was Paul—and to remember that he had apparently succeeded Paul as the primary leader in the church at Ephesus.

The city was an important Roman enclave with a population of more than 200,000 people. It stood at a strategic crossroads between other Roman economic centers and was built around a valuable harbor located on a riverfront three miles from the open ocean.[1] It was the capital of the Roman province of Asia and housed the temple to the revered Greek goddess Artemis, or the Roman equivalent, Diana (see Acts 19:23-27). It was reverence for the goddess that caused Paul and his companions all the trouble they encountered in their early ministry in Ephesus. You can read about it in Acts 19. Interestingly, Artemis left an important mark on history and is still honored in that region to the extent that I recently stayed in the Hotel Artemis in Istanbul—2,000 years after Paul and Timothy operated in the region.

Paul planted the church there and remained in leadership for three years (see Acts 20:31). Apparently, Timothy labored alongside him since we read of him earlier joining Paul's team while Paul was at Lystra (see Acts 16:1-3).

In writing to or about Timothy, Paul would describe him as his son three times and as a brother twice. Each of these fond remembrances speaks of an abiding loyalty between the two men. Timothy remained loyal to Paul, even after succeeding him in Ephesus. A nice definition of loyalty comes to us from the Old Testament, "A friend is always loyal, and a brother is born to help in time of need" (Prov. 17:17).

A loyal disciple will be there for his or her teacher in the teacher's time of need. I can imagine Paul needing Timothy's loyalty and encouragement whenever he came under attack for his teaching. The same would go for your teacher when others may gossip about him or attack him; you stand firmly beside him. Beware of your speech that you always remain united with the one who launched you into your walk with the Lord or your ministry.

Often the teacher is older than the disciple—this was certainly true of Paul and Timothy. There will come a time when age begins to tell its woeful tale on your teacher. At that time you must remember to honor your teacher in the way that Scripture requires a son or daughter to "honor your father and mother. Then you will live a long, full life in the land the LORD your God is giving you" (Exod. 20:12).

The person who cannot afford to share honor with others is the ultimate loser. Ronald Reagan had a plaque in his office that read, "There is no limit to what a man can do, or where he can go, if he doesn't mind who gets the credit."[2] Those who are wise enough to credit the past are destined to learn from it and to build upon it. Those who cannot honor those who have gone before are simply in line to repeat whatever mistakes the past may have held.

Loyalty may be the most important dividend you can return on the investment another person poured into your life.

LIVE A RIGHTEOUS LIFE

Paul himself calls Timothy to live a righteous life: "Don't let anyone think less of you because you are young. Be an example to all believers in what you say, in the way you live, in your love, your faith, and your purity" (1 Tim. 4:12).

This seems so obvious, yet several times I have been wounded when I've discovered that one of my disciples failed to live righteously. Sometimes the behavior is simply rudeness toward those he or she serves or toward other members of the team. It may be moral misbehavior. Those problems tend to lie only in the heart of the disciple. They hurt, but I don't feel major responsibility for them.

However, the sin may be a mindset that causes a leader to lead from *position* rather than through *relationship*. This is dangerous and can turn a healthy ministry cultish. We've all seen authoritarian leaders and the rigid structures they create. People like this do great damage to the cause of Christ. Sadly, I've seen a few of my own disciples go down this path, usually to their eventual destruction. Perhaps worse are those who manage to hold together a ministry by lording it over others—they damage lots of people.

As Peter wrote, "Don't lord it over the people assigned to your care, but lead them by your own good example" (1 Pet. 5:3). This problem in the life of a disciple always causes in me a measure of self-doubt. I wonder where I went wrong in the process of handing off my values to this particular disciple. One of my life's fundamental building blocks is respect toward others even when they don't respect me, or my God. When I see or hear of a disciple treating others disrespectfully, I am personally wounded.

Ronald Reagan was perhaps the most soft-spoken president in the history of our country (can you tell that I admire him?). He did carry a big stick, but he spoke with respect and dignity whether addressing friend or adversary. Even the words, "Mr. Gorbachev, 'Tear down this wall!'" were spoken without anger and in a respectful tone. I recently read that he kept a paperweight on his desk that reminded him to show kindness in his speech. It read, "Gently in manner, strong in deed."[3] I hope those words always describe my life and those of my disciples.

As I write this, I am sitting in a hotel room in a country far from home. I've just completed three days of seminars in a church pastored by a former disciple. Sadly, he became its pastor only four days ago. He had originally planted the church a dozen years ago. Then, having raised a strong disciple, he entrusted him with the lives of the congregation. But last weekend the successor's adultery came to light and my friend was forced to step back into the church as interim pastor. Need I tell you that he is wounded by the experience?

Everything we did or said in the past few days was colored by the failure of a once-trusted disciple. The church is in danger of splitting. Staff members are heartbroken and sagging under the weight of constantly needing to explain the current state of the church. What should have been a joyous time together worked out, but it would have been much more victorious if we didn't spend it trying to repair breakage caused by a disciple who moved out of the range of simple righteousness.

Even as they pick up the pieces of that broken church, the leadership team is looking back to clues they missed along the way. The pastor who committed adultery had grown exceedingly authoritarian. He had combined all the church's small groups into one large and quite controllable entity. Odd answers to questions about the use of money cropped up along the way. Unrighteousness takes many forms.

As a disciple, you *owe* it to your teacher to live a righteous life. This is all about actions, not mere words. Remember, other people's lives depend on you.

Just last night a man thanked me for moving my family to Hawaii so many years ago. He said that if we hadn't moved, we wouldn't have brought a man to Christ who brought this person into Christ and helped him get free from drug addiction. This man went on to say that he had been contemplating suicide when his friend intervened. Again he told me that if we hadn't moved to Hawaii and made disciples, he would not be alive today.

This man's friend, my disciple, led a righteous life in front of him—righteousness enough to win a hearing. This new convert has turned his back on drugs and is looking for a way to serve in our church. You owe your teacher a righteous life and you owe it to him, or her, to live a righteous life in front of your own disciples.

STAY ACCOUNTABLE

Paul reminded Timothy, "Do not neglect the spiritual gift you received through the prophecy spoken over you when the elders of the church laid their hands on you" (1 Tim. 4:14).

There is an accountability that runs in two directions in that short passage of Scripture. Most obvious would be accountability to the Holy Spirit, as it is He who bestowed the special gift from God. Timothy is accountable to pay attention to his gifting and to use it to further the kingdom of God.

But there is also a secondary accounting that is due the elders of the church who laid hands on Timothy. These may have been fellow elders in Ephesus, or they may have been those men who "spoke well" of Timothy to Paul in Acts 16:2. In either case, Timothy owed them something for endorsing him toward his life's call.

One of the things he would have owed them, and that you owe the principal people in your life, was an ongoing relationship where they had true access to him. Paul was saying, "Allow them to continue speaking into your life and listen, *really* listen, to what they say." Some speculate that the church at Ephesus was actually a network of perhaps a couple hundred congregations. If this is so, then Timothy was a pretty important person at the time when Paul wrote to him.

Paul, on the other hand, was a prisoner awaiting trial in Rome. Yet, Timothy appears to have maintained an ongoing listening relationship with his former teacher.

If someone invested time and energy into you, they didn't do so alone. The Holy Spirit was involved in the process, and chances are good there were others who intersected both of your lives along the way. You owe these people, and the Holy Spirit, a constant accounting of the way you live your life.

The parable of the talents comes to mind here. Are you busy hiding your gift in the ground or are you in the process of doubling what you received? Have you given thought to doubling it again? Do you live and minister from the base of your spiritual gifts, or are you the product of the latest book you've read or of the latest seminar you've attended? We all need to pay attention to those gifts bestowed on us by the Holy Spirit when others invested their lives in us. Remain accountable to the investment made in you by others. Make your teacher proud of you by investing well the life and gifts you received!

LISTEN TO GOD

While advising Timothy, Paul contrasted communication with God to that of those who commune with evil spirits: "Now the Holy Spirit tells us clearly that in the last times some will turn away from the true faith; they will follow deceptive spirits and teachings that come from demons" (1 Tim. 4:1).

Do you listen to the Holy Spirit? Did your instruction from your teacher include sensitivity to the voice of God? Do you hold outside teachers and/or authors up to Scripture, or are you easily duped because something *appears* to work? Or, are you one of those people who are so unoriginal that you simply copy the latest ministry fad or follow whoever draws the largest crowds?

I want my disciples to question everything they hear and everything they read. My goal is that they hold every idea or program up to the Scriptures to verify its reliability. I like it best when our staff discipleship time becomes a place for people to question the veracity of some point made by an author we are reading. I like it even if it engenders conflict.

Times of questioning tend to shape our spiritual DNA far more than when we simply agree with everything we hear or read. When we instantly agree, we are only saying that what we've read or heard is something we already knew. When we disagree, we tend to forge a new position in the fire of friendly debate. That kind of questioning leads to creativity and innovation.

At some point, we must be people of the Spirit as well as men and women of the Book. If we go deep in the Word and walk closely with the Spirit, we will be innovators and will value innovation on our team. The innovation quotient is one way to assess your own sensitivity to the Lord. Again, the Old Testament gives insight into the things of the Spirit: "Trust in the LORD with all your heart; do not depend on your own understanding. Seek his will in all you do, and he will show you which path to take. Don't be impressed with your own wisdom" (Prov. 3:5-7).

This would include turning off the computer and your cell phone long enough to hear from God, personally, about the situations confronting you. You owe it to your teacher to be a person led by the Spirit with a Spirit-given discernment of the difference between truth and error.

Over my lifetime I've seen several ministries blast their way to popularity among masses of Christians. Most were blessings from God. However, a few have turned out to be hurtful to the Kingdom over time. The leaders operated either from their own flesh or from a spiritual base other than that of the Holy Spirit.

Early on, I would have a strange sense of what I call "spiritual nausea" when interacting with, or even speaking about, the people involved. It was just a feeling—nothing to act on—but certainly a warning toward caution. Inevitably these turned out to be valid warnings as the ministries and people involved came to a bad end. The negative feelings were a form of communication from the Spirit. I was being warned to remain careful of the input I was receiving at the time. I think you owe it to your teacher to stay alert enough to the Spirit that you never get caught in error.

Paul ends this part of his letter to Timothy with these words: "Stay true to what is right for the sake of your own salvation and the salvation of those who hear you" (1 Tim. 4:16). Remember that the salvation of others depends on your discerning and remaining true to what is right. Be a *discerner* of truth and error. Don't be a fad-follower—it is simply too dangerous.

TAKE ACTION

We spoke of this in an earlier chapter, but it is worth our time here. And, since this chapter is a reflection of a sermon by one of my disciples, I want to honor him by including his thoughts at this point.

My young friend pointed us toward another of Paul's admonitions to Timothy: "Fan into flames the spiritual gift God gave you when I laid my hands on you. For God has not given us a spirit of fear and timidity, but of power, love, and self-discipline" (2 Tim. 1:6-7). He pointed out two obvious messages in that passage. Both are easy to miss if you don't read with your spiritual eyes open.

The first is the encouragement to fan a spiritual gift into flames. The only way to do that is to pour oxygen on the smoldering coals. In other words, engage in ministry. We only get to know our spiritual gifts by attempting to bless others. You'll never prophesy if you don't share the thoughts you think God is putting into your mind. You'll never know a gift of healing if you are too shy to pray with a person complaining of sickness. You'll never know if you have a gift of teaching if you don't stand in front of an audience.

The young man preaching that day has yet to discover that he is a marvelous teacher and preacher. Yet, everyone around will say that they've heard few in their lives with stronger teaching gifts. He is still a little unsure of his abilities, which is a good thing, as it goes a long way toward ensuring humility. But when he steps up to the plate, he swings the bat with all his might. As someone who has poured into his life, I find myself his greatest cheerleader as I enjoy his success.

The second instruction Paul gave Timothy in this passage is to reject a spirit of fear, replacing it with a spirit of power, love and self-discipline. I believe that Paul is speaking of demonic influence when he speaks of a spirit of fear. We are to turn our backs on demons and embrace the Holy Spirit who bestows power, love and clear-headed self-discipline.

A few months ago, while I was in South Africa, a friend showed me a photo of a man cooking steaks one evening on his barbecue. Whoever flashed the picture picked up the red eyes and tawny shadows of four lions lying in the grass behind the chef. The large animals were hungrily eyeing either the steaks or the man cooking them. From the photo you couldn't tell if he was a brave griller or simply unaware of the danger stalking him. I think we sometimes tolerate fear without understanding either the danger or the spiritual forces it represents.

Returning to the sermon that kicked off this chapter, the preacher told of being challenged to move from a highly successful ministry in one place to take a job in an entirely different culture. He had personal reservations and fears. But, sensing this was a God moment, he chose a kind of self-discipline that made the move possible. He withstood the temptation brought on by fear to disobey God. Think about this for a moment: We tend to sympathize over fear, but it is really a temptation toward disobedience. And last time I looked, disobedience toward God is called "sin."

Since that decision to move to a new culture, the original job turned into something so large that he might not have moved if he knew things would lead where they did. However, the original self-discipline made it possible for God to move him under the faucet where He would baptize him with greater responsibility and greater blessing. Again, as his discipler, I am thrilled with the progression of events.

Most of the content of this chapter came through the eyes of a disciple suggesting he owes these things to his teacher. And standing in the role of the teacher, I can say amen to everything he taught that day. These five offerings are those that a disciple, quite literally, owes to the person who earlier has laid down his or her life to make a serious investment in disciplemaking. Please take them seriously.

Notes

1. "The Church of Ephesus," Philologos Bible Prophecy Research, December 19, 1998. http://philologos.org/bpr/files/e003.htm.
2. Richard Norton Smith, "Reagan at 100—Why He Still Matters," *TIME*, February 7, 2011.
3. Ibid.

CHAPTER FOURTEEN

WHAT ABOUT
PLAIN OLD FRIENDSHIP?

I f you've gotten this far into the book and stayed with me, yet you feel frustrated, that would be because you believe in what I am writing but there is simply *no one* to disciple you. This is rare, but it does occasionally happen.

If you are in that unique position, I have some good news for you. Jesus promised, "Where two or three gather together as my followers, I am there among them" (Matt. 18: 20). He was talking about two or three people gathering to pray, which actually makes this promise very strong. But aside from prayer, who would walk away from a relationship with another person where Jesus promised to show up *every time* you got together?

As I said before, I've never had anyone disciple me in any intentional fashion. I've discipled many others precisely because I was never discipled. However, I've enjoyed a few outstanding friendships; the kind the Bible describes—think David and Jonathan or Peter and John.

In each of these friendships, our purpose was to come together around Jesus Christ and allow Him "into our midst" to disciple both of us. I can point to four of these friendships, each of which included long walks, lots of coffee and some pretty random conversations. We talked of our families, our marriages, our hopes, our travel plans and books we had read. We complained about money and lusted after nice cars. In other words, this was pretty common guy stuff.

But Jesus and God's Word were integral to each of these prolonged friendships. Each friendship caused us to grow stronger in Christ. Each made me a better husband and father. And each made me more confident in who I am.

Sounds pretty good, huh? But it gets better. Each of these friendships also gave birth to at least one new ministry. Three of them actually resulted in churches being born—big churches.

RALPH MOORE

God will always work in friendships. Jesus will always show up when two or three gather in His name. Peer-to-peer relationships carry the blessing of God. But that is no reason to avoid intentionally making disciples whenever possible.

I think it is a good idea to remember that even as Jesus, the master discipler, worked with His people, He ultimately sent them out in pairs to practice ministry (see Luke 10:1). There is power in godly peer relationships.

This two-at-a-time in ministry is probably why you see Peter and John, as buddies, healing the lame man near the temple gate in Acts 3. And it would explain why the apostles sent the same two to explore and strengthen the ministry of Philip in Samaria (see Acts 8:14). We have to assume that Jesus went with them as they helped move the Samaritan converts into a Spirit-filled experience they hadn't enjoyed under the ministry of Philip. Peter and John had been close to Jesus as they walked the dusty roads of Israel. It was natural for them to maintain the bonds of fellowship after He ascended to the Father. This was even more natural since they were both filled with the Holy Spirit—the Spirit of Christ.

I am a great admirer of a man named Dawson Trotman, who effectively brought the strong heritage of disciplemaking to the attention of the American church back in the 1940s and 1950s. Trotman died young. He drowned trying to save another man's life. But in his relatively short lifetime, he discovered the possibility of two people praying others into God's kingdom.

In 1934, Trotman, a young convert himself, was asked to share Christ with a sailor named Les Spencer stationed in San Pedro, California. After Spencer's conversion, Trotman nurtured him through Scripture memorization. Spencer soon brought a shipmate into the fold and a movement began.[1]

Several young men came into relationship with Christ through the efforts of Trotman and Spencer.

After great success in evangelism, the pair experienced frustration that their converts often did not stick with their faith after leaving port. Their answer was to create simple discipleship materials and invent a relational process that would enable mature believers to disciple others. The process was all about one-on-one disciplemaking.

They were effective, according to *TIME* magazine, because "it was the beginning of a movement that Trotman called the Navigators. . . . That sailor converted a friend with the technique . . . and that convert in turn convinced another. Soon Navigators were spread across the seven seas. At one point during the war there were Navigators in more than 1,000 U.S. Navy ships and stations."[2]

That little literature publishing effort has grown. The Navigators now number more than 4,600 staff, operating in more than 70 countries in 130 languages.[3] Even the name, Navigators, was born of the narrow focus of the original ministry. Trotman and his friends focused on men *navigating* the seas (and the myriad temptations offered in seaports) of this world. They felt called to minister to navigators, or seamen, and could have had no idea that the ministry they launched would one day reach millions.

Two unknown men managed to touch many of earth's nations through their prayers and almost naively simple inventions. Later, evangelist Billy Graham would ask the Navigators to provide follow-up materials for those accepting Christ in his evangelistic crusades. This was an attempt to move Christianity from the crowd to the individual—to bring it into relationships between two or three people where support and accountability become quite meaningful. It was an attempt to bring it to a place where concentrated prayer is a real option.

The Trotman story stands to underscore Jesus' promise to join us when two or three get together in His name—and to answer whatever prayers we offer. It all began with the friendship between Dawson Trotman and Les Spencer.

Their story also serves to illustrate the nearly unimaginable strength of a disciplemaking continuum as their disciples made disciples of their own that soon did the same. The relationship between these two men also illustrates the value of two friends spending time in the presence of Jesus—even if no discipling is happening other than Jesus in their midst discipling them toward greater accomplishment in His name.

Notes

1. Betty Lee Skinner, *Daws: The Story of Dawson Trotman* (Grand Rapids, MI: Zondervan: 1974), pp 76-77.
2. "The Navigator," *TIME*, July 2, 1956. http://www.time.com/time/magazine/article/0,9171,891299,00.html.
3. "Who We Are," The Navigators. http://www.navigators.org/us/aboutus.

CHAPTER FIFTEEN

PROBLEMS YOU
WILL ENCOUNTER

Let's spend a few moments looking at problems you *will* face as a disciplemaker; then we'll move on to common complaints disciples often make about their teachers and groups.

Before we start, let me offer a piece of advice I've found useful. I think it is important that we always look at ministry and its problems much like we would look at a chunk of Swiss cheese. When eating the stuff, you address the cheese and not the holes. By the way, have you ever tried to chew on a hole in a piece of Swiss cheese?

I promise you will have problems anytime you do anything of significance. Just get over it and get on with the job at hand. While problems do happen, they are just problems, not the core of ministry. They are the holes in the cheese. But if you let them, problems can cause you to take your focus off the good and concentrate on failures and mistakes. Do this and you will miss the blessing of the Lord. So forget the holes and eat the cheese!

A LEADER CONFESSES

I've been making disciples for a long time and have probably faced every problem that you will. I normally disciple in groups, and I am currently involved with more than 40 people in various groups. I've had hands-on experience launching around 70 of my disciples as pastors. If there is a problem, I've probably lived through it. I don't pretend to have all the answers, but I do think the advice below could save you some headaches.

Confrontation
Fear of confrontation was the biggest problem I ever faced. Jesus told us that we should confront problems face-to-face

(see Matt. 18:15-18). But He didn't say much about how to go about it. Even if He had, I would still have cringed in fear whenever confrontation came my way.

I struggled with this for many years as a young man. I was fearful and couldn't bring myself to confront someone unless I was angry enough that the anger overcame my fear. However, when you confront in anger, you seldom win a spiritual victory. My history was that of mostly running away while occasionally attempting to solve problems by alienating valuable, if misbehaving, people. I was such a chicken that I was nearly 35 years old by the time I finally felt comfortable enough to confront a problem without anger as my platform for courage.

Eventually, I gained the benefit of two major influences that helped me learn to jump on problems while they were still small. The first was a church administrator we hired, even though he severely intimidated me. He was a great guy and extremely well qualified for the job. He even resigned an executive position at a large aerospace corporation to come work on our team. Though he was always humble and easy to deal with, his background and expertise still intimidated the coward that I was.

I thought of him as a kind of spiritual superman. This guy was afraid of no one. He could even confront an issue without offending the persons involved. And, he expected me to do the same.

Much to my discomfort, he constantly held my feet to the fire over confrontation. Whenever he caught me complaining about a person, he would ask, "So what did you say to them to help solve the problem?" As you might imagine, I grew more afraid of his questions than I was of most of the people I needed to confront. A healthy fear of that man drove me into the arena, and I finally learned to confront without anger.

The story gets better. I knew I had finally graduated from his schooling on the day I had to confront *him* in a business meeting. When I did, he called me out with a tinge of anger in his voice, "Am I being confronted over this . . . ?" My voice trembled as I struggled to answer, "Yes, you are." He then immediately backed down. He simply gave up whatever he was arguing for in deference to the person he had discipled to the point of taking on the master. When we talked about it later, I discovered that the fact that I had *fully* learned my lessons made him proud of me that day. It was one of the crowning moments of my life.

The second great influence on my problem was the book *The One Minute Manager*. I love that book, as it is the most effective guide to personal confrontation I have ever encountered. It is as respectful in tone as it is practical. I recently met Ken Blanchard, one of the authors of the book. It was thrilling to thank him for giving such a gift to the world. I told him what I am telling you: "Jesus taught me to confront, but Ken taught me *how to* do it well."

The general idea of this wonderful little book is to consistently offer one-minute praisings whenever you catch someone doing something well. The book suggests that you wander around trying to *catch* people doing right things. Those short praisings open the door of love toward the occasional one-minute scolding when you might discover that a person doing something wrong.

The glory of a one-minute scolding is that it is respectful and filled with integrity. Instead of deceitfully rubbing someone's back and sticking them in the ribs, the authors recommend openly confronting unacceptable behavior (not personality or character). You do this for 30 seconds, followed by another 30 seconds spent reminding them of your personal *need* for them and their good behavior in order to succeed in your own role.

This book is fantastic, and all my disciples have read it at least once. It is one of my 10 all-time favorite books. By the way, I've only skimmed the surface—you should read the book!

One of the problems you will face as a disciplemaker is that of confronting other people. You can count on it, so you need to learn to do it well.

Deserters

Paul and Barnabas suffered under the desertion of John Mark. Jesus witnessed the cowardice of His disciples at the time of His greatest need. And you will have people, whom you love and trust, abandon you when you need them most. Often they will forsake you for someone else's flashy ministry. Or they might leave over a petty dispute.

Sadly, I have much experience here but lack a lot of advice to pass along. In a nutshell, all I can say goes this way: "Get over it!" Deserters are better left alone because you usually can't win them back. If they do come back it will be of their own accord. And think about this—they weren't really with you or they wouldn't have left you in the first place. You read this exact description of deserters in the New Testament, where we are told, "They never really belonged with us; otherwise they would have stayed with us. When they left, it proved that they did not belong with us" (1 John 2:19). Sad but true!

Teachers of False Doctrine

There will always be false teachers, and they will interrupt your relationships with some of your disciples. Paul described these people as follows:

> The kind of people who smooth-talk themselves into
> the homes of unstable and needy [people] . . . who,

depressed by their sinfulness, take up with every new religious fad that calls itself "truth." They get exploited every time and never really learn. These men are like those old Egyptian frauds . . . who challenged Moses. They were rejects from the faith, twisted in their thinking, defying truth itself. But nothing will come of these latest impostors. Everyone will see through them, just as people saw through that Egyptian hoax (2 Tim. 3:6-9, *THE MESSAGE*).

He describes these false leaders as teaching a counterfeit message designed to win the confidence (and perhaps the money) of unsuspecting believers.

The upshot of Paul's answer here seems to demand a willingness on his part to simply take the hit and wait until God exposes those false teachers for what they really are. My experience has shown me that these kinds of people are often too slick for open confrontation. Your role is to remain solid as a brick so that you're still standing after they fall. This often requires painful patience but pays off in the long run—and we're in this for the long run.

A Broken Heart Over Other People's Problems

This is a tough one. It is a hard calling to love others and bear their burdens, crying when they cry and laughing when they laugh. It may be tough but it *is* doable. And it is one of the reasons I disciple people in groups—I want to share the pain with a team of others. I simply can't manage it all myself.

I mean that last phrase literally. Recently, my friends and I have been praying for four church members who were in the process of losing their homes to foreclosure. The good news is that two were able to restructure their loans and the others are slowly winning the battle. The battle, of course, being the larger condition of the companies they each own. The bad news is that all this weighs on my heart like a ton of lead as I feel strongly called to pray for each individual.

Did you notice that I used the word "called"? I'm *not* called to pray for everyone who asks. Oh, I do pray immediately after being asked, but usually drop the burden right there. I simply have too many people in my life to carry all their burdens. But from time to time I feel called to bear someone else's burden in my own prayer life. If I let too many people onto my personal prayer list (and into my heart), I don't function well.

But I've shared the burdens I just mentioned with my mini-church. I believe there is strength when we join with others in prayer. I know it spreads the burden and makes life easier for anyone doing it. We need to share prayer burdens among groups of people. This is why the New Testament records numerous "one anothers" as it teaches us to organize the ministry. We are called to encourage one another, instruct one another, pray for one another, and so on. This is a team effort from start to finish.

Our church is organized around nearly 200 disciplemaking circles where people pray for each other, among other activities. I want them to bear each other's burdens so that none of us has to go it alone.

OTHER PEOPLE'S GRIPES

Here are a few of the complaints that people often *rightly* level toward the leaders of disciplemaking groups. Each is worthy of our attention.

If you are like most disciplemakers, you may sometimes find yourself more focused on the results than the process. Unfortunately, that kind of thinking will cripple you as most results come hand in hand with the process. When people bring reasonable criticism my way, it is usually when I have allowed results to take my eyes off of the relational process that actually gets the job done.

"Our Group Doesn't Meet Often Enough"

This is a big one. I have a brilliant friend who is well known and well liked in the Honolulu business community. He came to me with a vision to start an evangelistic disciplemaking group. He planned to start this with three other believers plus their pre-Christian friends. I thought it was a great idea. At least I did until he got into the particulars of his plan.

He insisted that since business people are quite busy he would hold the meetings only once a month. Sounds good on the surface, but his plan was lousy when it came to fellowship. If a person missed a meeting, he or she missed fellowship for two months. Besides, once a month with perfect attendance would still keep people from ever really getting to know each other.

The group lasted exactly two months before it died. Sadly, he thought it was the fault of flaky people. I think it was the result of diluted fellowship that never allowed people to feel they truly belonged. There simply wasn't anything to belong to. My friend cared more about his structure than he did about his people.

In contrast, another man launched a lunch-time church on Wednesdays in the business core of Honolulu. He began by gathering three friends and a couple of others invited by his friends. They meet weekly and have grown into a congregation of 100-plus people. Due to the generosity of a downtown real estate firm they move (rent free) from one unoccupied location to another. Even the constant moving doesn't seem to disturb the strong fellowship they've developed in this brown-bag luncheon church. By the way, did I happen to mention that more than 40 percent of their people attend no other church?

I often hear people complaining about infrequent or even randomly held meetings. Their complaints reflect an honest desire for real and consistent spiritual nourishment. Don't let this happen on your watch.

"I'm New, and I Don't Feel Included in the Group"

This one is serious. If you don't overcome this obstacle in a hurry, you never assimilate the newest people into your group.

The simplest answer to this objection is to stop whatever you are doing and do a round-robin introduction whenever a new person comes to the group. Do not single out the newbie and make him or her introduce himself or herself. Ask each person to share a little of their personal story. Spend the entire session sharing testimonies if you must. Do this and you will assimilate new people with ease.

Start by introducing yourself and go around the ring asking each person to tell who they are, why they are in the meeting and a short testimony of where they are with God at the moment. Also ask them to describe what, if anything, they are currently doing in ministry. If you are discipling a group of new believers be sure to make this process simple enough that a pre-Christian is not put off with a lot of church-talk. And be sure to ask the pre-Christian to share only as much as is appropriate to their situation.

This may feel frustrating because it draws you away from the intended content of the meeting. It will especially feel that way if the group is growing rapidly. You'll feel that you are not getting much done while spending so much time on introductions. But you'll find that it's worth the time you spend if you quickly make the outsider into an insider. And your people will be practicing their testimonies to the point that it gets easier for them to share their story outside of the group in evangelistic encounters.

"There Is too Much Socializing and Not Enough Content"

This can be a real deal-breaker. I had a red-hot group of twenty-somethings going in my living room a few years ago. Then my life changed and I handed the group off to a friend. The group went from studying the Bible, C. S. Lewis and Francis Schaeffer to doing nothing but hanging out and goofing off at my friend's house. They were all about food and fellowship and little else. The group fell apart within five weeks.

On the other hand, the second ministry item mentioned in the list in Acts 2:41-47 is fellowship. It comes right after teaching and just before prayer in the list of Early Church activities. I think of this as a kind of priority list. If I am right, fellowship is very important to the disciplemaking continuum. We need to keep our disciplemaking groups content-centered (apostles' teaching) but rich with fellowship. Mix the two well and you start to enjoy an effective prayer relationship (the third priority in that passage) in your group. By the way, food gets a big mention in that Scripture passage. I've found that food and fellowship do mix well.

"Our Prayer Requests Often Turn to Gossip"

Wow, this one hurts the most because it is too often true. People often use "prayer requests" as a mild cover-up for gossip. Some things may need to be prayed over, but only in a context where they do not constitute gossip.

My experience with this, coupled with my desire to use time efficiently, has brought me to a place where I like to do away with prayer requests entirely. This is because they often result in either gossip or simply praying about stuff not directly related to people in the room. I don't really want to pray about Aunt Jenny's cousin's cat.

Our rule is this: We each pray aloud at the end of the meeting, but we only pray about things that came up during our fellowship or in the course of our discussion. If it isn't important or personal enough to make it into our discussion we'll let someone pray about it on his or her own time. This way, since we challenge any gossip during the discussion, we've already kept our prayer time from being another form of backbiting. We're also confining our prayers to life's more important issues.

"I Never Get to Say Anything; Two People Do All the Talking"

This is another very real problem and requires you to show strength as a leader. Even stronger self-discipline is required, if you are like me—often the worst offender.

We sponsor the Alpha program in our church. As I write, we are finishing our twelfth Alpha series. We usually begin with about a dozen tables seating eight people each. We meet for dinner, fellowship, a video teaching by Nicky Gumbel and finish with discussion and prayer. Our problem is the fall-off rate. We'll start with about 100 people, but within three weeks that number will shrink to about 65. When we noticed the shrinkage was all during the first few weeks, we took a closer look at what we were doing. Much to our relief we discovered we weren't losing a few people from each table but losing entire tables. It didn't take long to diagnose the problem—table leaders who did all the talking alienated their members. Once we resolved that issue we solved the problem.

We always try to set up a mini-church or other disciplemaking group around a homework assignment—something they each heard in last weekend's sermon or a book they've chosen to read together. You can even simply ask each person to share something they got from their devotional Bible reading during the past week. If someone starts preaching, give a kindly reminder that time is limited and you want to be sure that everyone gets a chance to share. If they don't take the hint the first time, meet with them privately and ask them to help you keep the discussion moving. Giving a person this job usually solves the problem. If all else fails, be blunt, but do so privately.

If you find that you are the problem, take heart—it is normal for people to look to an established leader as the answer man or answer woman. But it is hurtful if you take on that role. I am often the worst offender if I don't maintain a high level of self-discipline. My problem may stem from having founded the church, but it is still a very real problem when people look to me for all the answers.

I've found two options to my temptation to do all the talking. The first is to simply turn any question I'm asked back to the group—let them collectively answer it instead of me coming up with the "best answer." They'll grow from the experience. The second tool in my kit is to discipline myself to never speak more than 10 percent of the time while we meet together—this is tough but doable.

"Our Group Is Simply Not Relational"

This happens when we become so content-focused that we forget the ultimate goal is teaching people to minister to each other. The first goal of disciplemaking is for ordinary believers to bring ministry to each other—it isn't the job of the leader to do everything. If all we ever do is discuss content, we are missing the real substance of disciplemaking, which is learning to "follow me, as I follow Christ." Remember that Paul was asking Timothy to follow him into ministry as he, himself, followed Christ into ministry.

This process is all about relationships that are centered around content but relationships still. A leader's role in this type of arrangement is "to equip God's people to do his work and build up the church, the body of Christ" (Eph. 4:12).

"My Group Is Not Open to New People"

If you are the leader, this one is your fault—even if you want it to grow but your people do not. Get busy and teach your disciples that Jesus calls each of us to be fishers of men and they are missing their calling if they think they can have more fun when they don't invite others to the party.

We've learned that there are three levels of group membership. The first is weakest: "I am committed to attend and be fed by the group." The second involves a little sacrifice: "I'll contribute time and even money if it is comfortable for me to do so." The third level reflects true discipleship: "I am committed to the vision and values of my group and will make whatever sacrifices necessary to see the vision accomplished." Level-three members are willing to engage new people—and they are willing to part with old friends to form new groups when the original gang gets too large for effective fellowship.

Now here is where it gets sticky: as the leader, it is your job to move people into level-three commitment. Seeking God for vision and communicating it to your disciples is primary to a leader's job. I like the *Amplified Version* of the Bible when it says, "Where there is no vision [no redemptive revelation of God], the people perish" (Prov. 29:18).

The point of having vision is to line up with the redemptive purpose of God. Redeeming lost people should certainly fit into anything we do in God's family. As a leader, this often means cajoling people to think higher thoughts and caring for others more than they care for themselves.

A healthy discipleship group is too good a thing to keep to yourselves. It needs to be shared; and the only way to keep sharing is to keep multiplying. We find that easiest to do when the leader takes one or two with them to start a new group. Who leads the established group when they leave? The leader's primary disciple, of course!

By the way, if you are the one instigating the closed mind, grow up and look to grow your group.

"Our People Often Skip Meetings—They Seem Apathetic"

This is the great danger of any group that continues for an extended period of time. People begin to take the meeting for granted, overlooking the fact that others are dependent on them for spiritual growth and vision.

This problem often occurs in our longer-running minichurches and even threatens our staff meeting from time to time. If you face this problem you need to act like a leader and establish some ground rules for the group. Lay out thoughts like, *Miss so many meetings and you are out.* Learn to set priorities for the group.

This is a pretty simple problem to solve. You just have to help people schedule their priorities rather than try to prioritize their schedule. If your meeting is important, it goes to the top of the list. If it isn't that important, they should get out.

A side note is disciplemaking groups that hive off new groups on a regular basis seldom face this issue. They are always filled with anticipation and excitement as new people come and they spawn new groups. In short, vision incites interest and enthusiasm.

"Our Leader Seems Unprepared for Our Meetings"

This usually happens in groups where the leader is cast in the role of a teacher whose job is to bring a new message to the group each week. There is already a downside to this approach in that one message tends to cancel out another if they come too close together. People who listen constantly to Christian radio will seldom be able to tell you what they heard two days ago—the more recent message cancels the earlier one.

The same problem occurs within the confines of a local church. Hear a sermon on Sunday and another on Wednesday and you probably won't remember the Sunday message by Thursday. Revisit the Sunday message on Wednesday and you'll remember it for months to come. The great benefit of this approach is that you get to assume the role of discussion leader rather than teacher, which brings me to the second problem associated with lack of preparation.

The second downside is that most leaders are busy. It takes time to prepare a message, and your average plumber or lawyer is probably too time-pressed to come up with a teaching that can rival what people hear on the radio every day. The small group as a preaching/teaching ground is simply impractical.

On the other hand, if you are all discussing your lives in light of a pastor's sermon, the leader can hardly come unprepared since the pastor did all the heavy lifting for him or her. In this same vein, if you use my idea about everyone reading the same book and discussing what the Holy Spirit said to each person through the book, life is easy on the leader. The role of a leader changes from that of a constant flowing fountain of wisdom into a pastor whose job is nurturing sheep in a small group. And you might note that healthy sheep beget more sheep.

IT'S WORTH IT

There are problems associated with disciplemaking, and these problems won't go away by themselves. You must work at them. However, nothing worth achieving is accomplished without problems.

Jesus called a bunch of fishermen and other assorted followers during the early part of the Gospels. Because He was young, they were probably right around His age. He often lamented that they simply weren't getting the message or that their faith was too small. Yet they touched off the greatest movement the world can identify today. They were worth the time He invested in them and they produced results that wildly outshone the petty bickering and confusion they displayed while walking the dusty roads of Galilee.

The Christ-followers who fled the persecution of Saul of Tarsus in Acts 8 turned into (unnamed) church planters by the time we read of them in Acts 11. They were literally running for their lives, yet they kept on doing the thing that caused them to flee Jerusalem in the first place—teaching others about Jesus.

Add in a scary miracle, and Saul their former tormentor became a pastor in one of their churches. He did this on the way to growing into the only apostle whom the Scripture describes as making disciples, outside of Barnabas.

Of course, Barnabas later split with Saul because he believed in John Mark while Saul washed his hands of him. The kicker is that Paul, writing from prison in Rome, later asks Timothy to bring Mark to him, as he "will be helpful to me in my ministry" (2 Tim. 4:11).

I like those words of Paul's. They describe nearly every discipling relationship I've ever had. At some point, I've wanted to give up on just about everyone. Yet, in the end, I see them as "helpful to me in the ministry." Not just *the* ministry; like Paul, I have to say, "in the ministry God has given to me."

WHY SOME SMALL GROUPS WON'T, DON'T AND CAN'T WORK

I hope you understand that I am holding on to hope that you get involved in leading a small group of *hungry* disciples. So why on earth would I write a chapter about why they don't work? It's pretty simple—they often don't. I want to explore why small groups often won't, don't and can't work. Then I want to point you toward a better way.

Fads come and go in the church world. I've lived long enough to have once read a magazine article titled, "The Church Without Sunday School Buses Isn't Growing." How many Sunday School buses currently ply the roads of your town on a weekend?

I remember when we all thought Billy Graham would win the world while we quietly went about our business. Billy faithfully held the gospel banner high, but that didn't win a culture to Christ. Then there was the cell church movement (something I see in Acts 2, and which is at much of the core of this book). For some reason that movement largely stalled, though there are still many cell churches around, including my own congregation and most of the churches we've planted.

Recent times brought on a couple of decades of focus on mega-churches. Now some are experiencing a backlash against the impersonality of mega-churches. This backlash is at least partly responsible for giving birth to a rising movement of simple churches (think house churches that may or may not meet in houses). Who knows what will come next?

DVDS DON'T CUT IT

Mega-churches will be with us for a long time to come, but the leaders are rethinking their approach to ministry. A courageous study recently came out of Willow Creek, one of the nation's largest churches. These people had the guts to professionally rate their success in the area of disciplemaking. The results were disappointing but enlightening.

200   RALPH MOORE

In the preface to the book, *Move*, Bill Hybels wrote about the disappointment engendered by the survey:

> We got one of those wake-up calls that you'd rather not get but you know you can't ignore. Our initial interest in conducting the survey was based on our long-held overarching hypothesis that increased participation in church activities—small groups, weekend worship services, and volunteering—increases a person's love of God and others. Said another way, Church Activity = Spiritual Growth.[1]

Hybel's anticipation pretty much reflects what the rest of us think: more activity results in more spiritual growth. Even I one day awoke to the realization that one person whom I saw at every function of our baby church was, in fact, still a baby Christian—after 10 years in the faith. Sadly, more participation—including small-groups—doesn't automatically result in growth. And the news gets worse. Hybels went on to reflect:

> Once we got over ourselves and let the data do the talking, we learned three shocking facts about our congregation: (1) Increased participation in church activities by themselves *barely moved* our people to love God and others more; (2) We had a lot of dissatisfied people; (3) We had a lot of people so dissatisfied that they were ready to leave.[2]

The study did reveal that more activity equates to greater spirituality in the early days of a person's walk with Christ, but that the results fall off later.[3] Unfortunately, those survey results are not confined to Willow Creek. More than 250,000 people have now taken the REVEAL survey, which produced the data, and the results are widespread. The findings probably fit your church and mine.

I admire Willow for exposing their problems for the world to see. However, I strongly disagree with one of the conclusions arising from this study, which is that small groups don't result in strong disciples. I'll get into that shortly, but bear with me while I vent a frustration. When the REVEAL survey results first came to Hawaii, some were preaching that small groups were a waste of time, based on what they read in the published results. To a degree they were correct—*some* small groups don't cause spiritual growth. However, other groups are very effective. I think the difference is in whether or not the group succeeds in getting people to reflect on Scripture.

My thoughts are pretty simple: Build a meeting around an edited-down, shorter version of a weekend sermon on DVD and you won't get much in the way of spiritual, relational or equipping results. Loading up on head-knowledge doesn't result in spiritual maturity. It is this model (which started with the mega-churches) that failed, not the concept of discipling people in small groups. The Great Commission isn't about programs, folks. It is all about disciplemaking relationships that are centered on life where it intersects with Scripture. The REVEAL survey speaks to this indirectly:

> We find that Reflection on Scripture is much more influential than any other practice by a significant margin. In fact, for the most advanced segments—Close to Christ and Christ-Centered—it's twice as catalytic as any other factor on the list. This means it has twice the power of any other spiritual practice to accelerate growth in spiritually mature people.[4]

A small-group model built around applying the sermon to a person's life will differ greatly from just another Bible study or a mini-sermon delivered via DVD or some other method. Discussing how a teaching fits into the person's life easily dovetails with personal Bible reading and the everyday issues of life.

WE DON'T NEED ANOTHER SERMON

One of my friends told a story that illustrates the need for people getting together, around Christ, in small groups. Please remember that when the Church was born, the believers met in homes as well as the Temple. Each place offered different functions toward the process of discipling nations. Some ministry functions work well in a large auditorium while others work better with people seated around a table sharing a meal. We need to operate in both settings. Here's the story . . .

A member of our church staff was on vacation in the southern part of the United States. His family joined an old acquaintance from our church for dinner. That man invited his new pastor along with the pastor's daughter. The church this man pastors is quite large and is a member of a prominent denomination.

The dinner topic rolled around to methods for doing church. The Southern pastor described how hard he worked to prepare sermons for three services a week plus a lesson for an adult Sunday School class. I need to point out that our staffer originally found the Lord in our church and had *never* been exposed to such a program-heavy approach to ministry.

When he was taken aback by the pastor's description of all the energy being spent preaching and teaching, our staff member blurted out something to the effect of, "So your adults get four teachings a week, is that true?" When the pastor said it was so, my friend asked him how much time he put into study.

The pastor's daughter volunteered that she personally spent five hours preparing to teach her own Sunday School class. The pastor said he put more time than that into *each* of his three sermons (one each for Sunday morning, Sunday evening and a midweek service) and his Sunday School class. Both seemed satisfied with their efforts and somewhat proud of the sacrifices they were making for the kingdom of God.

Our staff member, without thinking, asked, "Do you expect your people to actually get something from all your work? Do you think they really *implement* all that you teach?" Taken aback, the pastor replied, "Of course we do!" At that point, the pastor's daughter, perceiving disrespect in my friend's questions, got angry and left the room in tears.

Our staff member meant no disrespect. He was honestly shocked by the pastor's schedule and its effect on his congregation. My friend then asked the pastor if he didn't think that people only retained one sermon until they heard the next. The idea is that one life-changing message will cancel a previous one if they come at an individual too closely together. The pastor reluctantly agreed that this may be the case, and if it was so, he was spending many hours in unnecessary sermon prep.

My friend went on to describe our assumption that you can only fully absorb one life-changer every seven days. We actually believe this is linked to the Creator assigning one day out of seven for rest and meditation in the Old Testament, and for New Testament churches gathering "on the first day of the week" (Acts 20:7; see also 1 Cor. 16:2).

He further described how our cell groups focused on making disciples by discussing how their lives intersected with whatever the Holy Spirit said to each person through the pastor's sermon the previous weekend. He added that we then support each other in prayer about whatever the Spirit reveals to each individual. And he mentioned that these midweek meetings are seasoned with much food and fellowship.

The discussion with this pastor wandered back to the fact that the adult children of our mutual friend had recently left that pastor's church though they had originally embraced it with much enthusiasm. They said they left because they felt they were not getting fed. That really set the pastor aback. He is a man of integrity and was pouring his life into his sermons with all the energy he could muster. He was all about feeding the flock. To hear that people felt he wasn't feeding them spiritually hurt him deeply.

But it was a good hurt. By that I mean the pastor had an epiphany that was strong enough to sponsor change in his approach to his job. The church still has adult Sunday School, but only one sermon each weekend. They now meet midweek for fellowship, food and disciplemaking in homes throughout their small city. Did I remember to mention that those young people who left the church have happily returned and now *lead* one of the disciplemaking groups?

REASONS FOR SMALL GROUP FAILURE

Earlier, we discussed the fact that disciplemaking groups built around shortened videos of sermons don't cut it—too programmy and not relational enough. You might as well just throw in another church service in the middle of the week. In each case, the new message cancels the previous one in its effect on an individual life. There are other reasons why attempts to create disciplemaking groups in a local church fail.

Following the Crowd

One standout reason for failure is if your motive is simply to follow the crowd. This is the tragedy of the cell church movement of the 1970s. A few people had success imitating those early Christians on Pentecost. They then wrote enough books and ran enough seminars that the idea quickly gained all the momentum of a fad. And fads tend to run shallow; people failed because they only learned "how" to do cell church, but failed to understand "why."

The "why" is all about deepening relationships and disciplemaking with the intention of equipping *every* believer to do ministry, with some ultimately traveling to the ends of the earth to accomplish their call. This is about much more than disseminating information. It is about sharing life, even to the point of one man I know calling his mini-church leader at 2:00 AM so that his leader would talk him out of entering a sex-bar. Fads don't generate that kind of trust.

Just an Addendum

Another reason small-groups fail is that they are often an addendum to the church. In other words, they become just another program. They are not seen as centrally important to the mission of the church. If the command is to make disciples, that activity should be central to everything we do as members and leaders.

As I've repeatedly said, in our congregation we do two things differently than most. First, we look at every convert as a potential missionary we can effectively train through our local congregation and its disciplemaking process. The point is to make disciples all the time and to shoot for the moon in our expectations.

Second, we identify the senior pastor as the prime mover behind our disciplemaking effort, which for us centers around our mini-churches. We make jokes about the mini-church being the true church while the weekend services are church conventions. Corny but effective at helping people understand our mission.

In-reach Trumps Outreach

Some churches fail at small groups because the groups are all about what I call "in-reach" instead of "outreach." Our groups do *not* exist so that people will grow in the Lord. Of course, spiritual growth is one element we desire, but it is only a small part of a greater whole. We don't do much evangelism through small groups, so that isn't what I refer to when I discuss outreach.

What I mean by outreach is that every group exists to equip every member to accomplish his or her role in the Great Commission—outside the confines of the church. This keeps people from coming for selfish reasons. They come for equipping and strength that they can take outdoors into their everyday lives.

Most of our growth comes through the front door of our church—that is, the weekend services. People evangelize their friends, bring them on the weekend and they filter into home groups from there. But the weekend and the midweek always hold hands around the task of equipping every member for ministry. We are always looking outward. We want to equip ordinary people to effectively evangelize in their everyday lives.

Lacking a Culture of Sponsorship

Finally, some small groups fail because they fail to grasp a culture of sponsorship whereby the stronger leader is always on the lookout to advance the ministry of those under their care. Think here about Barnabas sponsoring Paul when the apostles still feared him. And then be sure to remember Barnabas sponsoring Paul when he went to Tarsus to bring Paul into the leadership circle in the newly formed church in Antioch (see

Acts 11:25-26). Finally, note that the "Barnabas and Saul" relationship eventually turned into that of "Paul and Barnabas." Barnabas was willing to relinquish leadership to his maturing disciple when it became obvious that God had a stronger anointing upon the disciple than upon the discipler.

A form of sponsorship is that of identifying strengths and weaknesses, then learning to help build the strengths. Think of a football team where the kicker is usually the smallest guy on the team. He could play no other position. But he does have the skill that makes him the person who *always* scores the most points over a season. It is easy to overlook someone because he or she doesn't compare well with someone else. It is harder, but much more rewarding, to identify strengths where God has hidden them.

The simplest form of this in our church arises in the need for a leader to replace himself or herself with one of his or her apprentice leaders when he or she moves on to start a new group. But sponsorship goes further than that. It may come in the form of helping raise funds for a group member to participate in an overseas mission. Or it may be something closer to home like the people in our congregation who have planted a small church in a skid-row neighborhood. Several of our mini-churches are gathered around them in a beautiful way, each finding a way to sponsor one or more of their converts. They do the usual things you would expect of a skid-row ministry—they collect soap and shampoo from hotels on business trips. They provide used clothing and bring food to share at church meetings.

But much more importantly, they actually make friends with the people who come in off of the streets. Some have even hired their new friends to work in their companies. In other words, they develop *real* relationships. This goes way beyond the feel-good stuff of soup kitchens. These people attempt to sponsor those in their circle of concern on to a productive life.

So there are valid reasons why disciplemaking groups won't, don't and can't work. However, the solution to each is pretty simple. It is all about intentionality. If you are committed to the opportunity, you will work out the obstacles that threaten you with failure.

Notes

1. Greg L. Hawkins and Cally Parkinson, *Move: What 1,000 Churches Reveal About Spiritual Growth* (Grand Rapids, MI: Zondervan, 2011), p. 16.
2. Ibid., pp. 17-18.
3. Ibid., p. 19.
4. Ibid., pp. 117-118.

CHAPTER SEVENTEEN

A FEEDBACK LOOP
THAT WILL
KEEP YOU RELEVANT

I don't know if you noticed this, but you are getting older every day. And it is a problem that simply won't go away no matter how hard you work out, or even if you are into Botox injections and pricey face-lifts.

All of my life I've been painfully aware that while older Christians will often follow younger leaders, the mass of younger people tend to turn off older leaders. This phenomenon is more endemic to Western culture than to Asia, but as American media exposure affects the world it will soon be a worldwide issue. The generation gap is usually rooted in the fact that younger folks are caught up in the latest fashions and musical trends, and because they have an irksome tendency to think they are reinventing the world as a better place.

I can remember a long while back when I *knew* very well that everything we did was new, revolutionary and would change the Church for the better (actually, that was somewhat true as I came of age in the midst of a revival). But even as the revival passed I *thought* I knew better than my elders.

REMAINING RELEVANT

However, in the midst of turning my back on everyone who had gone before, I couldn't ignore one man: Nathaniel Van Cleave. He came to pastor our church while I was in high school. Later, he accepted the position of president of the college I attended. And later, in the role of a bishop, he appointed me to my first pastorate. But none of those roles were responsible for my willingness to learn from this man.

Van Cleave did three things that kept my attention, even in my most rebellious moments. First, he intentionally surrounded himself with younger people. He stacked his staff with youth at every turn. Second, he actually sat through meetings *listening* to the young men he was discipling—he made disciplemaking into a two-way street. And, third, he somehow let those younger people *keep him relevant* to our generation. This took form in the cars he drove and the clothes he wore and so on. He was one of those rare individuals who could relate to younger people, wear current fashions and yet not look like an old kook trying to keep up with the kids.

Dr. Van Cleave had managed to establish a feedback loop that kept him culturally relevant well into his 80s. I knew him from his early 50s until he passed away more than 30 years later. After a lifetime of pastoral ministry and denominational oversight, he spent his final years teaching the Bible to very young Christians in a large youth-oriented congregation in Southern California. This man never got old. His body aged but his spirit and soul remained vibrant and connected to the future.

I'll never forget the day I was looking out the window of my high school architectural drawing class and saw this incredible man drive by in his new Alpha Romeo. He had picked the sedan instead of the sports car. But this was a time when few Americans drove foreign cars, and he had picked one of the coolest vehicles on the planet. Yet, he maintained enough restraint to go for the sedan, not the roadster. As a 16-year-old, he had me hooked. I decided that day that I wanted to be like Dr. Van when I grew up.

My focus has always been on raising leaders who are younger than me. Today, I disciple a couple of teenagers who long to be pastors. They are part of a seven-member group that includes a couple of pastors and a 78-year-old former church planter. The older man is the revolutionary who spends his Sundays goading aging pastors to pay attention to younger people in their midst.

The young men in that disciplemaking group are special. They are extremely talented but also wise enough to know that they need to learn from those who have gone before. However, what makes the group unique is that the older people see the wisdom in sacrificing their time for the sake of the very young. And their friendships with the rising generation keep them young in their thinking. They form a positive feedback loop with the wisdom of years blending nicely with the insights of youth.

THE NEXT GENERATION IS OF VAST IMPORTANCE

I confess that I get a little nauseated at slogans like "Next-Gen" or "Generation Next." That terminology appears to have been invented by people who are very much out of touch with the people they are trying to reach. However, I do believe that the most important mission of the Church is to evangelize and disciple each rising generation. This isn't only important today. It was always important and always will be. If we don't reproduce ourselves in younger people, the Church will cease to exist.

It is for this reason that I constantly teach the older people in our church that our job is to make disciples, finance the future and learn to enjoy music that may be foreign to our taste. I'm talking about the way we must operate at a whole-church level, not just in disciplemaking circles. If we fail to invest in the future, today, all of our efforts and energies will come to nothing within a few years of our own day in the sun.

Our abilities to engage the next generation keep our church viable, growing and capable of multiplying itself at home and on foreign soil. This is all about fulfilling the Great Commission. But it stems from the second commandment—loving our (younger) neighbors as we love ourselves. Did you notice that several of your neighbors are significantly younger than you?

IT GETS PERSONAL

Like I said earlier, I want to be like Dr. Van Cleave when I grow up. And five decades later I'm still growing up. I no longer surf because my arms are too weak to catch a wave, and age has helped change my taste in clothes. I even confess that I still drive a convertible while the kids are into pickup trucks. But I spend most days hanging out with people younger than myself.

I see my role in their lives as threefold: First, I disciple them; second, I run interference for them when they cross swords with older people in our congregation or with our staff; and third, I *learn* from them. They see the world through different eyes and their ideas fit today's world so much better than mine do.

I get to impart values to younger people while they impart innovations and inventions to me. "As iron sharpens iron, so a friend sharpens a friend" (Prov. 27:17). This is a very productive two-way street and the place I've chosen to live my life.

WHAT ABOUT YOU?

I once heard a prominent pastor announce that he was called only to reach his own generation and local community with the gospel. He was very effective at what he did and grew a congregation of a dozen people to more than 10,000. But he was only successful at exactly what he had said he would do. He reached his own generation in his own locality. He did not plant churches in other localities, and his congregation is slowly giving in to the ravages of old age.

He never intentionally made disciples. And though he did hire younger staff members, most of them left him with a sense that he had been more of a stepfather than a dad to them. From my vantage point, his was a life of constantly missed opportunities. After he retired, the church sadly and slowly slipped backward to about 30 percent of its former size—and it involves mostly elderly people who worship each weekend. The man did what he promised, and sadly it all caught up with him in the end. He hadn't raised a generation of younger leaders to take the place of himself and his peers. He is not able to reap what he did not sow.

I am told that there was a time, in the late 1940s through the 1950s, when people thought it spoke well of a person if he was seen as irreplaceable. If a church fell apart when its founder died, the general opinion was that he was so successful that he could not be replaced. I believe just the opposite. I think a person who was irreplaceable was an utter failure at the Great Commission. He simply didn't heed the words of Jesus when it came to making disciples. We should view ourselves as infinitely replaceable. And this is where you come in.

Though I'm a pastor, I'm not just talking to pastors here. What I have to say applies to every Christian. Do you remember when I mentioned three levels of commitment? Well, we should all be at level three. And if we are those people who are willing to make personal sacrifices for the cause, we *will* make disciples. It is just not that difficult. You simply have to care enough to obey the Master and love people around you. Invest yourself in others and you will leave a lasting legacy.

The pastor I just described as unwilling to reach beyond his locality and his generation and was a friend and sometimes a mentor to me. But whatever I gleaned from him always came at my instigation. I can't remember a single time when he reached out to coach or instruct me of his own volition. I owe him a great deal. But he could have left so much more behind had he made a simple decision to go beyond his own generation and his own community.

You are infinitely replaceable but also infinitely reproducible if you choose to reproduce yourself in younger people. And you will certainly stretch your glide by doing so. If you choose to hang out with younger people, you will learn from them while you pass on life's lessons. Doing so creates a feedback loop that will keep you relevant. Choose to invest your life listening to young people while you teach them and you will "grow tall in the presence of God, lithe and green, virile still in old age" (Ps. 92:13-14, *THE MESSAGE*).

Remember how I started this book by telling the story of learning how to make disciples by watching a 16-year-old boy disciple my young brother-in-law? Well, that is a process I hope to continue until the day I die. And I hope it is something you will learn to do as well.

CHAPTER EIGHTEEN

GOOD THINGS *DO*
COME TO AN END

Remembering the young man who taught me so much about making disciples requires that I tell you one more story. We hit a rocky spot in our relationship that brings me to the thought that things don't always turn out exactly as we would wish.

WHEN DISCIPLES LEAVE YOU

If you remember, what I learned from him was partly that I had already been *informally* discipling him and his closest friends when he took my brother-in-law under his wing. It was through observing him that I learned the *intentionality* of making disciples. But then, after six years, our relationship was suddenly cut off.

He grew strong in the Lord and became an effective Christian leader during those six years we spent together. As he grew up, I knew he was considering pastoral ministry. I also knew he was looking to attend a local college where I had graduated. It mattered little to me that he followed in my footsteps, but it apparently mattered much to him. In fact, it mattered too much—he didn't know how to handle our relationship after he decided to attend a different college. That choice of schools drove a wedge between us. One day he appeared in my office tearfully announcing his decision to attend the other school 500 miles away from where we lived. A half-minute later he was on his motorcycle heading for home. I didn't even get to say goodbye, he was just out the door. I never saw him for another year.

It was a year of confusion for me. I would have recommended the college he chose, so I didn't see that as a problem (though it *was* the problem—he felt he was betraying me by choosing that school over my alma mater). I spent the year wondering how I had offended him. And it wasn't only he and

I who were left hurting. All the kids in that youth group were left in confusion.

The story ended well. After a year, he returned home, attended a local college and we eventually hired him after starting the first Hope Chapel in Hermosa Beach, California. He came on as our youth pastor, and then became our very capable church administrator. He finally left us to plant a church and today pastors still another large Hope Chapel. He is successful in every way, and I am proud to be his friend as I watch him stretch his reach across oceans by sending *his* disciples to plant new churches in other countries.

What's my point here? That disciplemaking can and does often bring pain to your heart. If you love people, you are inviting them to hurt you; it is part of the package.

One of our earlier church planters became an archfundamentalist almost as soon as he launched his church. His theology grew more important than our friendship. His attitude toward me and toward our church got so bad over doctrinal differences that he actually told people we weren't even real Christians.

This was a man who had occupied two to four hours each week of my life for several years. We were good friends and I had invested a lot in his transition into pastoral ministry. Suddenly he was not only absent from my life, he was preaching that I was a heretic. We had several encounters over the next couple of years, but they always turned out badly. I was saddened and confused that such a good relationship could turn out so poorly. I did learn one lesson, however, and that is that relationships are more important than doctrine. Loving people is the second commandment after loving God.

Again, the situation eventually turned out well. Always a forceful man, one day he stormed into my office to demand that I listen to an apology. It seems that he hadn't slept for several nights and felt the Lord had told him that he never would sleep again until he made things right between us. I was so weary of the situation that I tried to brush him off when he came to apologize. He demanded that I hear him out. We became fast friends after his apology. By the way, we still differ over doctrine, but our respect for each other remains strong and he is a pillar in my life. The fact that we still differ in our thinking while loving each other is a testimony to the reality of Jesus in our hearts and in our churches.

Another of my disciples was the guy who perhaps embraced our values better than any other person I've discipled. But, a few years ago, he jumped into an adulterous relationship and of course broke off any contact with me and anyone else in our circle. He has since repented, is back with his wife and serving in another ministry. We are friends once more. But many people bore the pain caused by his sin and the greater pain of wondering if all the time invested in disciplemaking was really worth the effort.

The answer is that making disciples is always worth the effort, and anything worth doing is going to attract the attention of him who comes to "steal and kill and destroy" (John 10:10). But making disciples is always worth the effort and the pain.

IT'S BAD EVEN WHEN IT'S GOOD

If there is pain in things going bad, there is also pain when they go well. We should understand this, as each of us is called to take up our cross daily and follow Christ (see Luke 9:23).

I remember the day when I realized that I only had about 2,000 days left with my children before they would leave home for college. They were my closest disciples. The pain of inevitable separation began that day. I restructured my schedule to allow for more time with them. A cloud seemed to hang over my head during those few short months.

The hurt culminated the day before our oldest child flew off to college in the mainland. I was overcome with grief, sobbing uncontrollably for a couple of hours. It felt like I would never see him again. Of course, the first Christmas home from school made it all better, but the pain of separation was still real. And it was just as bad a year later when his sister moved off to the mainland to enter her college career.

Every time a disciple moves away or moves out to plant a new church, I go through separation anxiety. I know that even though the relationship will stand until eternity, it will never be quite the same.

One of my closest disciples over the past few years married our children's church pastor. He then joined our staff as our high school pastor. That brought the two of them even closer to my wife and me. We enjoyed many holiday dinners with them in our home. We even vacationed together. Then they left to assume the pastorate of a small struggling church.

I remember the first holiday when the wife came for dinner while the husband couldn't make it because of church duties. The little church was growing, and while what he was doing was thrilling, the fact that he couldn't join the old crew for dinner wasn't.

Today, the church they pastor has grown larger than ours. We partner in many projects and pull off some incredible seminars. But he has "graduated." Our relationship will *never* be quite the same—but that's the point of making disciples. They are supposed to change in their own lives. And they are to go and make disciples of others. By the way, with this man, our roles have reversed, and I am learning lots from him.

I know pastors who can't face the anxiety that comes with their disciples growing beyond the initial discipling relationship. Some even compete mercilessly with their disciples. One church in our neighborhood used to teach that anyone leaving the congregation where they met the Lord was walking out of the will of God.

I even know of a pastor who starts well, partners well and then seeks to disqualify his disciples as they come to a point of leaving the church to start another. Another pastor I know refused to allow his strongest disciple to plant a church within 40 miles of his; he even threatened to call him a "spiritual stepson" instead of a son if he did so. None of these people have learned that separation anxiety is a normal part of the process. We just need to learn to handle it with grace and dignity.

BIBLICAL EXAMPLES OF SEPARATION

There are several examples of disciples being separated from their masters. For instance, Elisha saw Elijah ride off to heaven in a fiery red Corvette. Samuel was taken from David through death. But a couple of these examples stand out as stronger models for us.

Moses and Joshua

We first meet Joshua when he is described as "Joshua son of Nun, who had been Moses' assistant since his youth" (Num. 11:28). In another place we read, "The LORD would speak to Moses face to face, as one speaks to a friend. Afterward Moses would return to the camp, but the young man who assisted him, Joshua son of Nun, would remain behind in the Tent of Meeting" (Exod. 33:11).

Joshua must have progressed well since he earned the right to lead the Israelites into battle with Moses supporting him from a nearby hilltop (see Exod. 17:8-13). Sometime later we gain further insight into their relationship as Joshua, *alone*, accompanied Moses down the mountain after his master had received the Ten Commandments on Mount Sinai (see Exod. 32:17).

But it is the sunset years of their relationship that can teach us the most important lesson about the inevitable separation of disciple and discipler. Moses *publicly* endorsed Joshua, in view of all Israel, as his successor: "Be strong and courageous! For you will lead these people into the land that the LORD swore to their ancestors he would give them. You are the one who will divide it among them as their grants of land. Do not be afraid or discouraged, for the LORD will personally go ahead of you. He will be with you; he will neither fail you nor abandon you" (Deut. 31:7-8).

It was Moses' gracious acceptance of the end of his own trail coupled with the public endorsement of Joshua that would help the people accept their new leader. Perhaps more important, Moses' words would stay with Joshua during times of difficulty. Separation can, and should, be a positive experience.

I recently handed off the role of lead pastor in our congregation to my son. We never planned for my successor to be my son—he earned the job in the eyes of the congregation before the leadership acknowledged that he was the person. He is bringing growth that I never could have envisioned. He's tightened up our statements of vision and values and is driving them deep into the hearts of our people. The results are amazing. The Lord is with him as He was with Joshua and Moses before him. I am terribly proud of him as his father, but I cannot finish this book without reminding you that he was also my disciple, though he is now my pastor.

Jesus and His Disciples

Jesus' disciples (learners) graduated. They became apostles (sent ones). It may have taken them several years to leave Jerusalem after he had commanded them to go, but they eventually went.

The result is that a third of the population of our small planet worships our Lord at this time in history. Those original guys did go to the ends of the earth as they understood geography at the time. Meanwhile, Jesus went to the right hand of the father. Separation anxiety was definitely a big deal to them, even after the miracle of the Resurrection. The pain will always be there, but it isn't necessarily bad.

What I am trying to say is that you picked up this book for a reason—a good reason. You understand that the Great Commission applies to you, personally. That the call to make disciples of all nations starts in your own neighborhood, perhaps in your own family. And hopefully, you understand that it extends from your local coffee shop quite literally to the remotest parts of the planet.

You can, and should, make disciples. You never know when you are going to function as a Barnabas to someone's Saul and that your seemingly feeble efforts are going to result in an entire culture being transformed.

My advice in one sentence: "Go for it!"

COULD OUR CONGREGATION
SPAWN A MOVEMENT?

My wife and I started a church with 12 people way back in 1971. Fortunately, it happened at a time of great upheaval in America—which made it easier to experiment with new ideas. The sexual revolution was upon us. Universities openly bristled with drugs for the first time. Our cities ruptured over racial issues and conflicted feelings over an unpopular war in Southeast Asia.

As a generation of high school students, we were influenced to question authority. By the time we hit college, the fruit of that influence permeated the culture. In those days, "overwhelming" authority was the preoccupation of student America. The country would never be the same after the late 1960s and early 1970s. A few years into the revolution, a handful of friends joined my wife and me to launch a church. We were primed for rapid change. Our church would certainly be different from the one that birthed it.

On top of our devotion to change, the Holy Spirit interfered. Two strangers, on two different occasions, "prophesied" that our church was going to be different from anything we had known— so different that we shouldn't bother to pray about it. We were just to expect something different. Not given to personal prophecy, I ignored the first "word." But when another person said exactly the same thing to me in an entirely different location three months later, I took notice. But that is all I did.

THE BIRTH OF HOPE CHAPEL

The "new thing" happened as we launched a church plant from our fledgling congregation. The new church met in a home. The pastor was bi-vocational, and he had no formal training. The lack of education was a big log for me to crawl over. In fact, when the group first broached the idea, I flatly refused to support it. I only became convinced of the possibility after the Navigators recruited the potential pastor to serve as a missionary in another country. If they believed in him, why shouldn't I?

Aside from the narrow channel of my mind, the other obstacles were denominational. Our group had a rule against two
churches in one city, and there were already two of them re-
senting one another for breaking the rule. Adding a third
could only cause more conflict.

Our denominational bylaws *required* formal education for
pastors. This guy had no "credentials," so we had to pull a rabbit out of a baseball cap to pull off a new church. No formal
credentials, maybe, but he did bring impressive assets to the
project. He was *successfully* leading five Bible studies each week
besides heading a strong family and running his own business.
The issues of salary and building were no problem. He earned
good money in finish carpentry on upscale homes. The group
met in a house so they didn't need a building. Besides that,
they had a line on an empty space they could rent if the new
congregation grew—it was a bar. Finally, the rookie pastor and
I had a strong relationship, we were so close that you would be
hard-pressed to discern who was discipling who.

Anticipating institutional reticence, we decided to go with
that wonderful proverb, "It's easier to gain forgiveness than
permission!" We started the church and then informed the denomination. To our surprise, they embraced the baby church
like parents who overcome skepticism about their kid's marriage at the sight of their first grandchild. They even paraded
us before several thousand people at their convention to tell
how a local church had birthed a congregation—something
that hadn't happened in decades.

Our church was called Hope Chapel. The new congregation dubbed itself "a Branch of Hope." I balked. I wanted them
to remove the word "hope" from their name. I feared criticism
for starting a denomination within a denomination. They kept
the name.

Within weeks, a second congregation spontaneously unfolded among a number of newly saved Jewish-American students at Santa Monica City College. We'd become a movement in incubation—almost without choice. Those "prophecies" were coming to fruition. We had stumbled into something so new that we couldn't have imagined it. We, quite literally, would not have known how to pray for it because we had no vision for it.

OUT OF CONTROL MULTIPLICATION

Now, many miles down the road, I've still only personally started one youth group, planted two churches and had a direct hand in multiplying just over 70 church plants from the congregations that I pastored. Somewhere along the way, the multiplication process got out of control. Those few churches have become a *movement* that keeps generating new congregations. To date we can identify more than 700 church plants. Each is a direct relational outgrowth of those original 12 people in a Southern California beach town. (We do not count churches where we simply encouraged another group to begin multiplying churches. These are direct descendants.)

In New England, we can identify growth that runs through nine generations of pastors each taking the baton from one leader almost simultaneously and passing it on to the next. We planted churches in Japan. And one man launched over 100 churches in Pakistan while being discipled long-distance by a businessman in our church. A young convert got the bug for church multiplication in our first couple of years. When I bumped into him years later, I discovered that he pastors a large church in South America and has multiplied more churches than the rest of our "movement." The thing is out of control—and that is exactly as it should be.

We don't govern churches. We've birthed congregations in a maze of denominations. Many are in our own church family, but most are independent congregations. In countries where persecution is an issue, some have banded together corporately in order to gain government protection.

This is all so loose that we can only approximate the number of churches. Even then we only attempt to tally numbers about every four years. We simply contact all the known churches in the network, asking, "Have you planted any new churches since we last spoke?" We get contact info for the newest churches and call them with the same question. As you can imagine, this has become a ponderous task. We last polled growth three years ago and are uncertain as to whether to even attempt it in the future. The only reason we ever counted in the first place was to force church multiplication onto other people's agenda in an era that saw mega-churches as the answer to the world's problems. Besides that, keeping count has helped us maintain a priority within the movement toward ongoing multiplication of churches.

THE CHAOTIC NATURE OF GROWTH

I used to feel pretty uneasy about the chaotic nature of what has grown up around the simple idea of multiplying our congregation. Then I read a book called *The Starfish and the Spider*. The subtitle says a lot: "The Unstoppable Power of Leaderless Organizations." The book describes the unsurprising death of a spider that gets poked in the head with a pin. It contrasts that to the resilience of starfish, which can survive just about anything. Most starfish will grow a new appendage (do you call them legs, arms or points?) if it is cut off. In one species, the severed appendage will grow into a whole new body.[1]

You get it! Each cell of that starfish carries DNA capable of reproducing the whole organism. I think that is how Christ intended His Church. Each member should be capable of re-producing the whole. The Early Church appears to have been a somewhat chaotic, nearly leaderless organization (unless you count Peter as the first pope and the Jerusalem Council as executive officers). But this was the genius of it all. I no longer cringe at the chaos of what has grown from our church. I now relish the extreme flexibility of it all.

My role in all this is pretty simple. My job is to keep an ideal alive. To keep people thinking that the unseen is more important than the seen. That what they could become is far greater than what they've been. That what they might accomplish has more to do with the ability of God to bless something than it does with their experience or their personal abilities. My task, as I see it, is to keep people focused on discipling nations rather than just building churches. My life goal is to stimulate others to plant movements instead of settling for just growing congregations or even planting a few churches.

Movements are dynamic and sloppy. They are alive, not static. Difficult to contain, they prefer pragmatism and innovation to institutions and traditions. They seek to inspire and empower rather than control people. Movements esteem teamwork and ordinary "heroes" above superheroes.

A denomination may be a movement, but usually is not. Similarly, gathering a bunch of pastors around a heroic leader may be useful, but a movement it is not. A movement procreates relationally through simple, easily reproducible models and systems. A movement sustains itself through multiple generations geographically as well as historically.

A HELPFUL HISTORY REMINDER

The Holy Spirit blesses movements. While the Twelve held council in Jerusalem, a bunch of unnamed people launched churches in Cyprus, Cyrene and eventually in Antioch. From Antioch the Spirit kicked off a church multiplication movement that would sketch the history of Europe and the Mediterranean.

After Rome fell, a young Englishman held slave to Irish tribesmen broke captivity when Jesus informed him of an escape route in a dream. Back home he converted to Christianity only to sense a call to carry the gospel to his former captors. Years later, Patrick traveled across Ireland, healing the sick and preaching God's kingdom as he made transit to the village of his former misery. From there, he discipled a nation.

A generation later, the Irish monk Columba launched a pitiful little boatload of 12 "brothers" into the Irish Sea with no particular destination in mind. They had a goal, but no destination. Once they reached deep water, they jettisoned oars and sail, trusting the Holy Spirit to take them wherever He could best use them. The sea could have swallowed them. It didn't. They could have died of dehydration in the middle of the North Atlantic. But they survived. Rocks as sharp as razor blades could have flayed them like Atlantic Cod. Instead they fell ashore on a rare sandy beach on the coast of Scotland. After evangelizing that nation, those motivated priests launched underground missionary raids, preaching and planting churches across the then post-Roman, post-Christian European continent.[2]

As movements go, the Protestant Reformation comes to mind, as does Puritanism in England and the American Colonies. In turn, England and the United States simultaneously birthed the great evangelical movement that we still identify with the worldwide growth of Christianity.

The underground church in China is busy launching its "army of worms" and sending secret missionaries into Muslim lands. The Christians in Nigeria have missionaries strategically placed in the post-Christian industrial nations of Eastern and Western Europe, and even Japan and the United States. As I write, the church grows faster in Mongolia and Nepal than in most other nations.[3] The Holy Spirit indeed specializes in movements.

SO, WHAT ABOUT YOUR CHURCH?

The sum of all of our goals will fall short of discipling nations. By that, I mean, if you could gather the strategic plans of every congregation, every spontaneous movement, even every denomination, the total of all their goals would fall short of total saturation evangelism.

Bummer! We should think bigger. We should be more responsible. We should this or that! But we can't. None of us is responsible for eating the whole watermelon of world evangelism. We can, however, reassess our situation. We could take another look at our disciplemaking processes. We could start to raise our sights simply by choosing to turn from leading a congregation toward attempting to lead a cluster of them. If I sound a little simplistic, so be it—simple works. This is ultimately a numbers game. If we all multiplied instead of adding, we would be farther down the road.

Your church as a movement will draw fire. Some will criticize. Others won't get their heads around larger goals. But it could happen—and it should.

Notes
1. Ori Brafman and Rod A Beckstrom, *The Starfish and the Spider: The Unstoppable Power of Leaderless Organizations* (New York: Portfolio/Penguin Group, 2006), p. 35.
2. John Eldridge, *Waking the Dead* (Nashville, TN: Thomas Nelson Inc, 2003), pp. 201-201.
3. Patrick Johnstone and Jason Mandryk, *Operation World: 21st Century Edition* (London: OM Authentic Media, 2005), pp. 451, 470.

AUTHOR CONTACT

Ralph Moore
c/o Hope Chapel Kaneohe Bay
45-815 Po'okela St.
Kaneohe, HI 96744

www.facebook.com/ralphmoorehawaii
www.ralphmoorehawaii.com

New Generations Need
New Churches

Do the Math. It's Time
TO MULTIPLY!

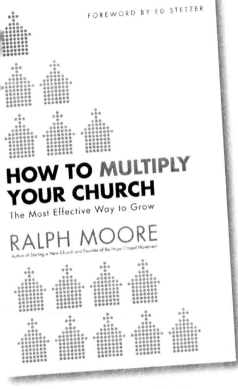

How to Multiply Your Church
ISBN 978-0-8307-5133-4
ISBN 0-8307-5133-5

Churches are bigger than ever, but their rates of growth can't keep up with population increases . . . existing congregations simply cannot add enough believers! The good news is that by multiplying—that is, by steadily and strategically planting new churches that, in turn, will plant new churches—the global Church can create more of what Ralph Moore calls "harvest points." In *How to Multiply Your Church*, Pastor Moore shows you why multiplication is the key to growing God's global kingdom, and he offers proven methods for how to implement multiplication in your community. *How to Multiply Your Church* is the next leap forward for those who long to see God's kingdom increase. Don't just add to your numbers . . . multiply!